Published exclusively for Metro Books by Gusto Company AS

© 2008 Gusto Company AS

Written by Rory Storm

Original concept by Gusto Company

Designed by Allen Boe

Illustrations by Miguel Coimbra, and public domain

ISBN-13: 978-1-4351-0194-4

Printed and bound in China

1 3 5 7 9 10 8 6 4 2

MONSTER HUNT

MONSTER HUNT

The Guide to Cryptozoology

RORY STORM

METRO BOOKS

NEW YORK

CONTENTS

INTRODUCTION TO CRYPTOZOOLOGY

"Whoever fights monsters should see to it that in the process he does not become a monster. And if you gaze long enough into an abyss, the abyss will gaze back into you."

– Friedrich Nietzsche

Cryptozoology is not a word that comes up in conversation very often. In fact, take a straw poll among friends and family and it's likely most people won't even know what it means.

The official definition according to Webster's Dictionary is:

"The study of the lore concerning legendary animals (as Sasquatch) especially in order to evaluate the possibility of their existence."

You might prefer to think of it as the search for hidden animals, ones that local people, rumors, and folklore say exist but for which there's no conclusive scientific or photographic evidence. Not yet anyway.

The most famous of the modern-day cryptids—the term used for these thus-far hypothetical animals—are Bigfoot, the Yeti, and the Loch Ness Monster, but there are many, many more.

The invention of the term cryptozoology (from the Greek kryptós *meaning "hidden,"* zōion *meaning "living being," and* logos *meaning "study"—literally "the study of hidden animals") is commonly attributed to Belgian zoologist Bernard Heuvelmans. However, Heuvelmans himself traced the scholarly origins of cryptozoology to zoologist Anthonid Cornelius Oudemans, who attributes the coinage of the term to a Scottish explorer named Ivan T. Sanderson. The term "cryptid" was eventually coined by John Wall of Manitoba, Canada in 1983.*

Hominid-*A member of the Hominidae ("great ape") family, including humans, chimpanzees, and gorillas— both living and extinct.*

Once the preserve of a slightly obsessive (and critics would say, wacky) fringe element, cryptozoology does have its mainstream supporters. Many scientists and zoologists are committed to using rigorous scientific methods to research and investigate cryptozoological animals around the globe. They argue that so much of the planet remains unexplored that there could be a myriad of new species out there. So, expeditions are regularly mounted both by scientists and amateur cryptozoology enthusiasts alike to confirm once and for all whether there exist creatures such as living dinosaurs, hairy hominids, or simply as yet undiscovered species in the natural world. The study of hidden animals has been pursued since ancient times when most of the population believed in mysterious monsters and bizarre beasts. In those days exploring and questioning the natural world was the calling of many respected scholars.

Today's men and women who are bold enough to study cryptozoology tend to be mavericks. Part scientist, part private investigator, and part explorer, the modern cryptozoologist risks the scorn of fellow scientists who prefer the firmer ground of conventional science. An inquiring mind is essential, as is an ability to fly in the face of received wisdom. Perhaps most importantly, the subject demands courage in the field.

The Mission of Cryptozoologists

Despite these common qualities, cryptozoologists approach their studies in a variety of different ways. Some are respected scientists in other fields who follow the accepted scientific prin-

Charles Hoy Fort (1874–1932) was an American writer and researcher of anomalous phenomena, that is to say, observed events, which lay outside the accepted theories and beliefs of the time. Put more simply, the weird and the wacky. Critics of Fort considered the study of spontaneous anomalies a pseudoscience, and they viewed him as gullible and naïve. Nevertheless, Fort compiled thousands of notes on unexplained phenomena ranging from teleportation and UFOs to crop circles and cryptozoology. In fact, so closely is his work associated with these phenomena that they are now collectively referred to as "Fortean" phenomena, or Forteana.

ciples of orthodox zoology in order to establish the existence of new species of animals. Others have a more unorthodox approach and are willing to follow hunches, go on wild goose chases if need be, ignore the skeptics, and continue believing that anything is possible.

Whatever their beliefs or research methods, all cryptozoologists are dedicated to the investigation of mysterious creatures as yet unidentified by science and which inhabit the world of native folklore and legend rather than textbooks and academic volumes.

Expeditions and Fieldwork

In order to carry out these investigations, researchers have to get out into the field, traveling into some of the most intimidating and remote areas of the globe armed with the latest recording equipment, such as video, digital, and film cameras, DVMS systems which shoot sixty photos per minute, night scopes, motion detectors, and (for the sea and lake monsters) underwater cameras and sonar equipment.

Television crews and magazine staff have also been sent on expeditions in search of the elusive subjects of local sightings, admittedly with a more cynical agenda. These crews rarely, if ever, produce any conclusive documentary evidence.

Yet, despite this stubborn lack of evidence, those who have seen, heard, or researched any of these astounding creatures still believe that they're worth pursuing, and that one day they will prove beyond a shadow of a doubt that such monsters exist.

Bernard Heuvelmans, a pioneer in the field of zoology, believed passionately that the scientific community should be more open-minded to the possibility of undiscovered animals. He argued that anecdotal stories and traditional accounts by non-European native peoples throughout the world had not been taken seriously in the past because of the West's confidence in its superiority, but that didn't mean that these accounts were not valid.

To illustrate Heuvelmans's claim, you might like to consider that local tribesmen had spoken of a man-like ape in Africa for centuries, a claim dismissed for its inaccuracy until European explorers discovered the mountain gorillas in 1902. Similarly, few people believed the stories Scandinavian sailors told about a huge sea monster that could grow twice as long as a bus, but we now know that the giant squid exists. So why can't there be other large creatures still undiscovered in the world?—that's the question that cryptozoologists would ask us to consider.

Cryptozoology enthusiasts also refer to the fact that many unfamiliar animals, when first reported, were considered hoaxes, misidentifications, or simply too strange to exist. Take, for example, the giraffe, which, when first discovered, was thought to be a combination of a camel and a leopard. That's why its scientific species name is *camelopardalis*, or "camel-leopard." Other now-accepted creatures once dismissed by skeptics as misidentifications include the platypus, the grizzly-polar bear hybrid, and the Komodo dragon, among others.

Logic alone cannot convince a skeptical public of the merits of cryptozoology. You are either prepared to suspend disbelief or not. You either support those who crusade on the fringes of science in their search for the elusive or you don't.

DISCOVERIES THAT KEEP CRYPTOZOOLOGISTS SEARCHING:

✘ In 1938, the coelacanth was found in a fishing net off the coast of South Africa. This "living fossil" is a representative of a type of fish that was believed to have been extinct for 65 million years. Although it was unknown to scientists, local fisherman knew the species well and called it the "gombessa."

✘ The megamouth shark was only discovered in 1976 after it became entangled in a ship's anchor off Oahu, Hawaii. Sightings of megamouths now number approximately one annually.

✖ The remains of a species of tiny human *(Homo flore-siensis)* were discovered in 2003, on the remote Indonesian island of Flores, taking the anthropological world by surprise. These descendents of *Homo erectus* lived just 18,000 years ago and were around when modern humans were colonizing the area. The unearthed individual stood just over 3 feet tall, with a grapefruit-sized skull. The local people of Flores told legends of a similar "creature" called Ebu Gogo, and stories of its existence persisted as late as the nineteenth century.

✖ Clouded leopards were the last of the big cats to be discovered in 1821, but in 2007 a new species of leopard was identified prowling the jungles of Borneo. Newly named the Bornean clouded leopard *(Neofelis diardi)* it's believed this species separated from the Sumatran clouded leopard *(Neofelis nebulosa)* 1.4 million years ago but it has taken until now to spot the difference. Genetic analysis and comparisons of fur patterns now show the two animals to be as distinct as the lion and the tiger, according to the World Wildlife Fund (WWF).

The discovery of the Bornean clouded leopard is further proof that all sorts of unknown creatures could be lurking in the Bornean jungles. Although many mainstream experts remain skeptical, science has demonstrated that certain mythological creatures were rooted in now verified animal species, and cultural tales and native traditions about unidentified beasts persist in every corner of the globe from Dartmoor to Delhi, and from the Congo to Canada. How can we be sure that these creatures don't exist? Come along on a monster hunt and let's see what might be out there.

Early explorers in Australia described kangaroos as creatures with heads like deer (without antlers), standing upright like men, leaping like frogs, and sometimes with two heads, one on top and another on the stomach. Small wonder no one believed them!

Clouded leopard

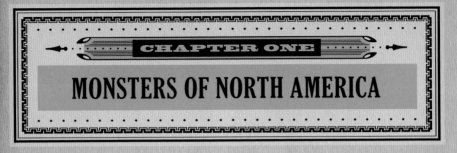

CHAPTER ONE

MONSTERS OF NORTH AMERICA

*"Either the most complex and sophisticated hoax in the history
of anthropology has continued for centuries without being exposed,
or the most manlike (and largest) non-human primate on earth
has managed to survive in parts of North America
and remains undiscovered by modern science."*

—Forensic anthropologist George W. Gill,
Former Director of the American Board of Forensic Anthropologists

Whether it's because Americans are especially observant or because ours is a continent full of wild open spaces, vast forests, and rugged terrain, North America appears to have more than its fair share of monsters.

They are not modern day phenomena either. Most of the cryptids described by eyewitness accounts conform to descriptions of cryptozoological animals that have been described by Native Americans and preserved in their oral history for centuries.

Sightings of lake monsters have been reported up and down the length of the continent from Texas to Vancouver, and North America even has its very own bird-monster that was the eponymous title of a famous 1960s British television show called Thunderbirds.

However, the most famous of all North American cryptids has to be the Bigfoot, a.k.a. Sasquatch, who has been the subject of numerous television documentaries and also the main character in a 1980s film *Harry and the Hendersons*!

Without further ado, let's learn a little more about the varied and exotic monsters of North America.

Sasquatch

The Sasquatch (also known as Bigfoot) is one of the most famous cryptozoological creatures. Many North American native tribes have immortalized Bigfoot for centuries, and its existence is not questioned in their societies.

The term "Sasquatch" was coined in the 1920s by American schoolteacher J. W. Burns. It is derived from a Chehalis word meaning "wild man."

Believed to be primarily nocturnal, the Sasquatch sleeps in temporary shelters constructed of leaves and vegetation. It has a loping walk and can run as fast as a horse in short bursts. Largely silent, it communicates by knocking rocks or sticks against hollow tree trunks. However, it does have a complex repertoire of vocalizations, and a phenomenally loud "scream" that several witnesses have heard when it is startled or hurt. Sasquatches are shy, gentle creatures that normally resist contact with humans and do not retaliate (see Bigfoot Abduction, page 27).

The "Bigfoot Hunter" character portrayed by David Suchet in the 1987 Steven Spielberg movie Harry and the Hendersons *is rumored to be based on René Dahinden who, in the 1950s and 1960s, gained a reputation as the most prestigious Sasquatch hunter in the field.*

The earliest written reports of these giant ape-like animals appeared in Western newspapers in the 1860s, and the Sasquatch only earned its nickname "Bigfoot" in 1958, after a road crew in California discovered some large footprints and took a cast of them.

MONSTER FILE:

Name: Sasquatch

Also Known As: Bigfoot, Skunk Ape, Cripple Foot

Size: Estimates vary but sightings and the North American Science Institute (NASI) put Sasquatch at around 7 feet, 7 inches, although some witnesses report a height of up to almost 15 feet. Estimated to weigh between 500 and over 1,000 pounds, with an average estimated weight of 650 pounds.

Footprints: The average footprint measures around 15.5 inches, but the longest measured is 27 inches long.

Home: The Sasquatch is principally associated with British Columbia, Canada, but sightings have been recorded in many remote areas across the United States and Canada.

Origins: There are two main theories. Many believe that the Sasquatch is a humanoid creature that has developed more slowly than the human race, but others firmly believe it to be an upright walking ape related to *Gigantopithecus*, an extinct giant ape.

Appearance: The Sasquatch is covered in hair, not fur, which ranges in color from black and dark brown to red, gray, and even white.

American and Canadian oral history abounds with stories of rural encounters with a tall, hairy, bipedal ape-like creature. These are not just the wild imaginings of local eccentrics—respected elders in communities have come forward as eye-witnesses and their stories have been taken very seriously in many areas.

In Florida, the Sasquatch is referred to as the "skunk ape" because of its awful smell.

In 1967, investigators Roger Patterson and Bob Gimlin shot a short film of an upright walking female Sasquatch as it paused in a clearing in Bluff Creek, California. The film shows the creature standing about 6 feet, 9 inches tall, with pendulous breasts. It glanced at the humans before moving off slowly into a stand of trees.

Although the film has been examined by numerous skeptics and experts bent on discrediting it, most agree that the film appears genuine and that, at the time, the technological skills were not available to make a suitably convincing, form-fitting costume, nor to produce a prosthetic capable of emulating the sophisticated leg and foot flexure displayed by the Sasquatch in the film. Patterson and Gimlin's film remains the most compelling argument for the existence of the Sasquatch to date.

In 1969, experts discovered a "man-ape" encased in a block of ice in the Midwest. They thought that they finally un-covered the evidence they had sought for so long to prove the existence of the Sasquatch. It had an ape-like toe but the padded feet of a human being. Mystery still surrounds the "Minnesota Ice-Man," as the beast was dubbed by the press, because it was withdrawn from public investigation before scientists could determine its origins.

In recent years, Sasquatch sightings have become less frequent—and there have been a number of high profile hoaxes. Some believe that, as human settlements expand

In 1970, a trail of 1,089 consecutive footprints was found in snow near Bossburg, Washington. The right footprint suggested the foot was deformed and had a missing toe—causing the cryptid footprint maker to be dubbed "Cripple Foot."

into more remote areas, the Sasquatch is losing its natural habitat and becoming extinct. Nevertheless, the consistency of eyewitness reports has many in the scientific world still wondering.

BIGFOOT ABDUCTION

In 1924, Albert Ostman went camping near Vancouver. One night, he noticed that his backpack had been ransacked but he dismissed the incident and went to sleep. In the middle of the night, Ostman was abruptly awoken as someone or something scooped him up inside his sleeping bag. There was nothing he could do as he was bumped and bounced along for several hours.

At daylight, Ostman realized that there was not just one captor, but four—three adults and a child—and they were huge, hairy hominids. These half-man, half-apes didn't harm the man but they kept him captive for six days. He was only able to escape after the oldest and biggest male became ill from eating some tobacco from his backpack.

Bobo

The Bobo is the local name given to a sea monster whose carcass washed up on Moore's Beach (now Natural Bridges State Beach) in Monterey Bay, California, in 1925. Thought by some to be the body of a plesiosaur (its neck was described as being about 20 feet long), it was postulated by others to be a rare type of beaked whale.

Plesiosaur-*A flippered marine reptile from the Mesozoic Era (248 million—65 million years ago), not considered a dinosaur. Plesiosaurs are divided into two groups; the group that most closely resembles the cryptozoological Bobo (and in fact many lake monsters) is the plesiosauroid, a wide bodied creature with a small head and skinny neck.*

Basilosaurus-*An elongated whale-like creature from the Cenozoic Era (65 million years ago to the present).*

MONSTER FILE:

Name: Bobo

Also Known As: The Monterey, Santa Cruz Sea Monster

Size: Around 30 feet in length

Home: The northern Pacific Ocean, off the northern Californian coast at Monterey Bay

Origins: Some experts believe that the Bobo, first sighted in the 1920s, is a descendant of the plesiosaurus or the basilosaurus, which became extinct millions of years ago.

Appearance: A huge silvery gray sea serpent with a round head, long neck, and spiny humps

Just days before the Bobo carcass washed up on the beach, a report was published in the *Santa Cruz Sentinel* of a "terrific battle" between a dozen or more sea lions and a monster fish. Eyewitness E. J. Lear said of the event, "I saw the water being churned to foam and thrown high up in the air. It was shiny and I took it for a big fish. A dozen or more lions were battling it, and every once in a while all would rise out of the water. It looked to me as though all the sea lions were attacking it beneath as the monster came out of the water several times. In telling of the battle of that night I estimated its length at 30 feet."

Just offshore from the Monterey Peninsula, the Monterey Submarine Canyon bisects Monterey Bay, plunging to 6,000 feet and encompassing a coldwater upwelling rich in nutrients and abundant in food supplies that could easily support sea monsters, according to crypto-enthusiasts. The near-shore presence of such a deepwater canyon within a semi-protected bay is unmatched anywhere in North America and many believe that the Bobo lives undisturbed in its depths.

In 1996, U.S. Marines caught a giant oarfish off the coast of San Diego. The 22-foot monster was metallic silver in color with a bright red stripe running along its length. These little-known deep-sea creatures have only been sighted alive about three times in a century and could easily be described as a sea serpent. Certainly this finding illustrates what a deep and mysterious place the Monterey Submarine Canyon is—deep enough to hide other creatures?

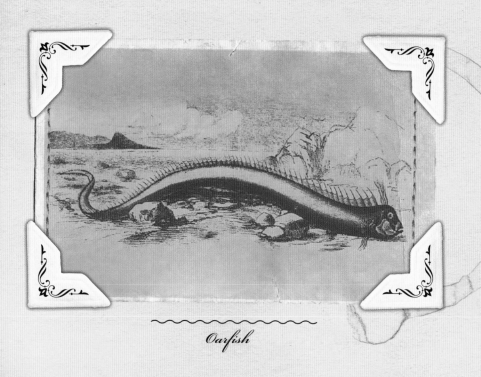

Oarfish

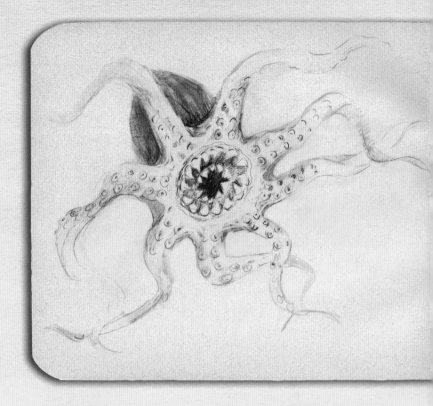

Devil's Lake Monster

Anyone who has ever visited mist-covered Devil's Lake in Sauk County, Wisconsin, can testify to its eerie atmosphere. Most are not surprised when they hear that sightings of a lake monster abound at Devil's Lake.

Tales handed down through generations of the native Nakota Indians tell of a huge creature with many tentacles that lives in the lake. The oldest account tells of a Sioux chief who took a hunting party of young warriors onto the lake one moonlit night. As their canoe slipped through the inky waters, a mass of giant tentacles broke the surface, capsizing the canoe and pulling the unfortunate warriors into the dark depths. The screams of the drowning men caught the attention of their fellow warriors onshore who witnessed the grisly event.

To pay homage to the victims—as well as to appease the demon of the lake—the surviving warriors held an annual festival during which gifts and animal sacrifices were made.

MONSTER FILE

Name: Devil's Lake Monster

Also Known As: M'de Waken (meaning "mystery" or "bad spirit lake") by the native Nakota Sioux

Size: Up to 20 feet in length

Home: Devil's Lake in Sauk County, Wisconsin

Origins: Similar to the giant squid

Appearance: Reddish brown with a long neck, small head, and large tentacles

During a year of particularly harsh drought, the water level of Devil's Lake dropped until it eventually became two shrunken lakes, separated by a shallow strip of mud running through the center. One morning, the Nakota tribe, which had stayed close to the drying lake, witnessed a vast, fish-like creature grounded on the narrow mud strip. The animal, which they described as having a long neck and small head, thrashed and writhed for several days but even the most courageous warrior would not approach because they believed it to be an Unktizina—an evil spirit—and they feared further reprisals. Finally, the beast worked itself free and slipped back into deeper waters.

Ogopogo

Certainly the most celebrated of the North American lake cryptids, the Ogopogo has gained notoriety with monster hunters worldwide.

The earliest reports of an Ogopogo sighting come from various Native American tribes from the region. The Salish tribe called it "the snake in the lake" (N'ha-a'tic) and the Chinook tribe called it "the great beast on the lake" or "the wicked one." All the tribes believed it to be malevolent, and Kelowna warriors would throw small animals into the lake as appeasement, hoping the creature would not attack their canoes.

As a test of bravery, Salish warriors would travel to Rattlesnake Island in Lake Okanagan, whose shores were littered

Name: Ogopogo

Also Known As: Naitaka, (meaning "sacred creature of the water"); N'ha-a'tic, (meaning "snake in the lake"); "the great beast on the lake"; "the wicked one."

Size: Between 15 and 20 feet in length

Home: Lake Okanagana, British Columbia, Canada. The majority of sightings, some as late as 2,000, have occurred just off Rattlesnake Island.

Origins: There are two schools of thought regarding the origin of the Ogopogo. Many eyewitnesses have described this creature as a smaller version of the plesiosaur-like Devil's Lake Monster (measuring 15 to 20 feet in length) while others believe it may be related to the extinct whale known as the basilosaurus.

Appearance: A dark gray, long-necked, snakelike creature with a head that bears resemblance to that of a horse or goat

with the bones and carcasses of animals that had been consumed by the monster.

In 1914, a group of Canadian Indians stumbled upon a decomposing carcass on the island, which many researchers believed to be the remains of a baby Ogopogo. Sightings have continued throughout the twentieth century and into this millennium. There is even hazy photographic evidence, in particular a photo taken by Ed Fletcher in 1976, showing distinct humps on the surface of the water, and some video footage filmed by Arthur Folden in 1968, which shows a creature of whale-like proportions rising out of the lake. However, none has been as dramatic as the latest sighting by Daryl Ellis in 2000 (see 80-mile Swim, page 36).

80-MILE SWIM

On August 24, 2000, cancer survivor Daryl Ellis attempted to swim the entire 80-mile length of Lake Okanagan in order to raise money for cancer research. When he reached the middle of the lake, Ellis claims that he witnessed two long, grayish-black creatures undulating beneath him in the depths of the lake. After about two hours of swimming alongside these creatures, Ellis started to get nervous so he swam to the spotter boat and got on board. Clearly shaken, Ellis refused to return to the water. Finally, he overcame his fears and re-entered the dark waters where he came up close to one of the monsters whose eyes were "as big as grapefruits."

Lake Okanagan

Manipogo

The Manipogo is a serpent-like lake monster that inhabits the relatively small body of water near the arctic coastline of eastern Canada. The creatures stay together after mating and the birth of their offspring, possibly in a pod similar to that of whales and dolphins, to tend to their young.

Not as famous as its British Columbian cousin, the Ogopogo, the Lake Manitoba monster known as the Manipogo has nonetheless received its fair share of sightings and attention. In addition to oral accounts, the first recorded sighting of Manipogo surfaced around 1908. There has been a steady stream of sightings ever since.

MONSTER FILE

Name: Manipogo

Size: Measuring from 12 feet to over 50 feet in length with a girth of roughly a foot

Home: Lake Manitoba, Manitoba, Canada

Origins: Researcher and writer Gary Mangiacopra believes that Manipogo may well be a leftover population of the zeuglodons that were thought to have died out millions of years ago. Roy Mackal, the famed Loch Ness Monster expert, supports this theory.

Appearance: Long muddy-brown body with humps that show above the water, and a sheep-like head

---

Most famously, the Manipogo was spotted and photographed in 1962 by two sport fishermen who noticed an unknown creature swimming across the lake in front of their boat. Richard Vincent and John Konefell watched it for more than five minutes before it vanished.

Zeuglodon-*A primitive elongated, whale-like creature that became extinct 30 million years ago and may have been able to crawl on land. The creature has recently been renamed "basilosaurus" although the name "zeuglodon" is still common among cryptozoologists.*

The image that the two captured that day shows a dark object about 12 feet in length protruding almost 2 feet out of the water. However, when Vincent was asked about his encounter in 1974, he was reluctant to say that he'd seen the Manipogo, preferring to report that he had photographed "something" in the lake. Some feel this indicates that his original assertions that he saw the Manipogo were untrue; others suspect that he was simply suffering the dispiriting effects of ridicule from cynics and disbelievers.

In 1997, the Toronto Globe and Mail *newspaper reported that a local farmer named Roulette claimed to have shot and killed a Manipogo. It was said that he hid its body in a nearby barn and was offering it for sale at a price of $200,000.*

Naturally, the tabloid press jumped on the story, alleging that the Royal Canadian Mounted Police (RCMP) had seen the creature—a fact that the RCMP officer involved in the event later denied. The prank was dismissed as the work of a practical joker, but some investigators remain unsure. The event served to renew interest among cryptozoologists in this elusive lake monster.

Despite several well-publicized hoaxes, there have been a number of Manipogo sightings, starting in the summer of 1999. Cryptozoological investigators are hot on the trail, looking for evidence that the elusive lake monster exists.

Eyewitnesses of lake monsters usually report an individual creature, but a group of seventeen witnesses, most of them complete strangers to each other, reported seeing a group of three Manipogos together, two large and one small.

Lake Manitoba

Mothman

The Mothman is one of the strangest and most terrifying cryptozoological creatures ever reported in America. Between November 12, 1966, and December 15, 1967, it terrorized citizens in the Point Pleasant area of West Virginia. Over the course of that year, more than 100 people reported seeing a 7- to 9-foot-tall black winged creature with glowing red eyes. Many said that they felt a malevolent force in its presence.

The sightings began when two couples, parked at an old World War II munitions dump site that the locals called TNT, say they were chased by a large creature. They reported the incident to the police, and the sightings continued from there.

Silver Bridge collapse, Ohio

Despite the relatively short but concentrated burst of reported sightings, this was not the first time such a fearsome creature had been seen in the area. Local Native Americans of the Iroquois, Tuscarora, and the Wyandot tribes have documentation that chronicles a large bird-man figure which they called "flying heads" and "big heads."

According to reports, the Mothman can fold its wings and walk on the ground with a strange shuffling gait, similar to that of a penguin. In general, it has not been observed flapping its wings, not even on take-off. It simply holds them straight and stiff as it glides, which eyewitnesses describe as unnerving. In most sightings, the Mothman is traveling much faster than any bird. Many victims site the Mothman during what seems to be its Mothman's favorite activity—chasing cars.

One young couple who were on a date told cryptozoologist Loren Coleman, who investigated the sightings and subsequently wrote the book, Mothman and Other Curious Encounters said that "they felt this thing attack them." Coleman said

Name: Mothman

Size: 7 feet tall with a wingspan of 7 to 8 feet

Home: The majority of sightings date from the mid-1960s in the Charlestown and Point Pleasant areas of West Virginia.

Origins: As the largest concentration of sightings have been witnessed in an abandoned ammunitions dump dating from World War II near Point Pleasant, many scientists believe the Mothman to be a mutation from a World War II experiment, living in the abandoned tunnels which riddle this largely impenetrable wilderness.

Appearance: A winged-man, gray in color with large reflective red eyes that appear to glow.

---

in a feature published in *USA TODAY* on January 23, 2002, that one of the pair told him, "A huge creature about 7 feet tall with huge wings and red eyes shuffled toward them, they ran to the car, and at 100 mph drove back to Point Pleasant. They could see the creature flapping right behind them."

In 1966, some eyewitnesses, including author John Keel, reported encounters with the Mothman where it spoke of a disaster that would visit the town in the near future. On December 15, 1967, one year after these encounters began, the bridge connecting Point Pleasant to Ohio over the Ohio River collapsed, killing forty-six people.

Although some believed that the sightings of the Mothman ceased after the bridge tragedy, there have in fact been subsequent sightings right up to the present day.

THE MOTHMAN PROPHECIES

Journalist John A. Keel's 1975 book, The Mothman Prophecies, *chronicles the story of the strange season of events in Point Pleasant. In 2002, a $42 million film of the same name starring Richard Gere was released, based on the book.*

In an interview with the Los Angeles Times *on January 23, 2002, Mark Pellington, director of* The Mothman Prophecies, *commented: "I believe in things greater than us that are unexplained. The mysteries of life are so profound; that is why this legend and other kinds of mythology exist. I feel it keeps us human."*

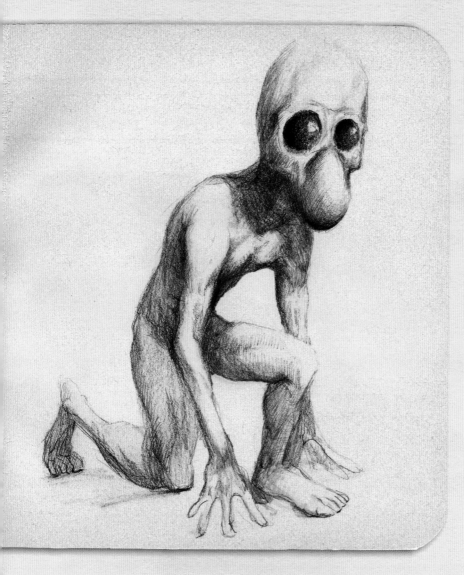

Dover Demon

O n April 27, 1977, residents of Dover, Massachusetts, a small suburb outside Boston, reported three separate sightings of a bizarre creature that was dubbed the Dover Demon by a local newspaper. Witnesses described it as about 4 feet tall, thin-limbed with a large oval head and two large, luminous eyes.

At around 10:30 p.m. seventeen-year-old Bill Bartlett was driving with two friends when he spotted "something" slinking next to a wall of stones lining the street. The thing turned it's head and looked directly into the headlights of the car. Bartlett swore he saw two large, shiny eyes glowing brightly "like orange marbles."

MONSTER FILE

Name: Dover Demon

Size: Up to 7 feet tall

Home: Dover, Massachusetts

Origins: Early ufologists speculated that the creature was an alien or some sort of mutant hybrid, perhaps created as a result of a human experiment. Others theorize that it is really a being from other dimensions, accidentally transferred into our world through a dimensional warp.

Appearance: The creature has a large watermelon-shaped head and illuminated orange or green eyes that resemble glass marbles. It has long, thin arms and legs with slender fingers that it uses to grasp the pavement. It is hairless and has rough flesh-toned skin described as tan and sandpaper-like. It has no nose, eyes, or mouth.

Ufology-*the study of UFOs (unidentified flying objects)*

Those who place themselves at the more scientific end of the cryptozoological spectrum have shown no interest in the Dover Demon whatsoever. They dismiss it as yet another spooky figment of people's imaginations that only serves to discredit the serious work of cryptozoologists.

However, less skeptical investigators believe that the eyewitnesses were entirely credible, and that there is nothing in their accounts to indicate a hoax. Investigator Loren Coleman, who lived in the area, was among those who interviewed the witnesses, along with ufologists Walter Webb and Ed Fogg. "We have a credible case, over twenty-five hours, by individuals who saw something," says Coleman in the 2001 edition of his book, *Mysterious America*.

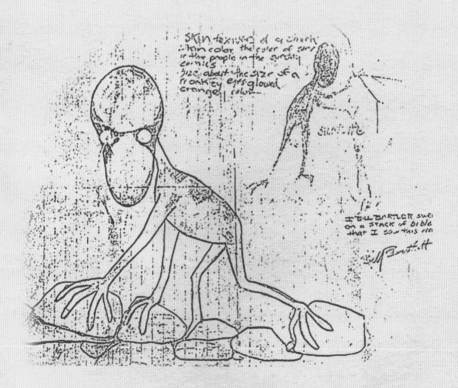

Although the other passengers in Bartlett's car did not see the creature, they did testify later that their companion seemed genuinely distraught. When Bartlett arrived home his father noted how distressed he was. Bartlett then drew a sketch of the being.

About two hours later, fifteen-year-old John Baxter saw a short figure walking down the road toward him. When it saw him, it stopped and fled into woods at the side of the road. John pursued the small figure, halting at the edge of a shallow gully. He looked across the gully at a tree, against which stood the figure. Claiming that he didn't know of the other sighting, he nonetheless described a creature similar to the one Bartlett reported.

The next evening, the creature was seen again, this time by Will Taintor and Abby Brabham. They desribed a monkey-like creature without hair that was thin and sat on all fours at the side of the road. Brabham reported that the creature's eyes were green.

For centuries, the Cree Indians have talked about a race of creatures called Mannegishi that live in or near water. They are said to often climb on rocks and ledges, and like to tip over canoes and small boats, drowning the occupants. They describe the Mannegishi as semi-humanoid, with very thin and lanky arms and legs and big heads minus a nose and mouth—exactly like the Dover Demon.

Gloucester Sea Serpent

Although sea serpent sightings occurred occasionally along the New England coast in the seventeenth and eighteenth centuries, it wasn't until 1817 that sightings of the Gloucester Sea Serpent in the harbor of Gloucester, Massachusetts (just north of Boston) became a seasonal occurrence.

In August, 1817, two women claimed to see a strange creature swimming in the harbor. Almost simultaneously, the captain of a coasting vessel saw the same sea serpent. Several days later, Mrs. Amos Story saw the monster through her telescope on Ten Pound Island while William Row reported seeing a creature which he described thus: "its head was as broad as a horse or more so, but not quite as long."

In total, there were eighteen sightings of the "sea serpent" that year. Most reports were very similar—a snake-like monster with a horse-sized head and about 60 to 100 feet long. They all commented on the fact that it swam with its head and neck vertical and with its "humps" streaming behind.

These sightings continued throughout the nineteenth century but they began to dwindle in the twentieth century with only fifty-six in total up to 1950 (compared with 190 the previous century). The last sighting in New England was off the coast of Marshfield, Massachusetts in 1962. Then, after over thirty years of silence, a report came from Fortune Bay, Newfoundland in 1997, that a creature fitting the description of the Gloucester Sea Serpent had been sighted.

MONSTER FILE

Name: Gloucester Sea Serpent

Size: 60 to 100 feet in length with a 3-foot girth

Home: The coasts of Massachusetts and Maine

Origins: Experts believe this elongated creature may be a remnant population of plesiosaurs that became extinct millions of years ago.

Appearance: A multi-humped serpentine creature with a head as broad as a horse and horn-like appendages protruding from its skull. It's gray in color and covered in thick scales.

EYEWITNESS ACCOUNTS

John Josselyn, an early eyewitness to a sighting of the Gloucester Sea Serpent, described her 1638 encounter with the creature: "They told me of a sea serpent, or snake, that lay coiled up like a cable upon the rock at Cape Ann; a boat passing by with English on board, and two Indians, they would have shot the serpent, but the Indians dissuaded them, saying that if he were not killed outright, they would all be in danger of their lives..."

In 1817, ship carpenter Matthew Gaffney shot at a sea monster as it neared his ship. He was convinced that he'd hit the Gloucester Sea Serpent, but it simply turned and looked at the boat and then sank beneath the surface of the water and disappeared, apparently uninjured.

Thunderbird

The densest area of Thunderbird sightings is the Black Forest region of Pennsylvania, where this huge bird has been spotted soaring above the sparsely populated forest and game lands.

The legend of the Thunderbird began with the Quillayute, a Native American tribe living along the Quillayute River. It is said that the Chief of the Quillayute called on the Great Spirit to save his people, who watched in silence as a huge Thunderbird with feathers as long as canoe paddles flew toward them with a live whale in its great claws. The Thunderbird left the people the whale and flew back to its perch in the hunting grounds of the Great Spirit, saving the Quillayute people from death.

The name "Thunderbird" derives from the common supposition that the beating of its enormous wings causes thunder and stirs the wind. The Comanche tribes call the Thunderbird "baa" and the Potawatomi Indians call it "Chequah." According to these and other tribes, the Thunderbird would soar down and seize its victim by the shoulders, carrying him or her away to be devoured on a nearby ledge or lofty perch.

MONSTER FILE

Name: Thunderbird

Also Known As: Baa, Chequah

Size: Sightings vary as being 2 canoe-lengths from wing-tip to wingtip, and between 15 to 18 feet.

Home: Mainly Pennsylvania and the Southwestern U.S.

Origins: Paleontologists reject the theory that a large and conspicuous bird such as a teratornis (meaning "monster bird") could exist in modern times but some believe that the extinct condor-like bird from the Pleistocene era (1.8-0.1 million years ago) could be the origin of the modern Thunderbird.

Appearance: Similar to an eagle or condor only much larger. It has black eyes and a rugged beak, huge talons, and thick legs, and is covered in dark grayish/brown or black plumage.

While sightings date from the earliest Native American times, sightings by settlers date from the 1840s and have been fairly consistent through the present. For a period during the nineteenth and early twentieth centuries, reports tended to describe a more pterodactyl-like creature, but now they have returned to the feathered, more condor-like descriptions given by early Native Americans.

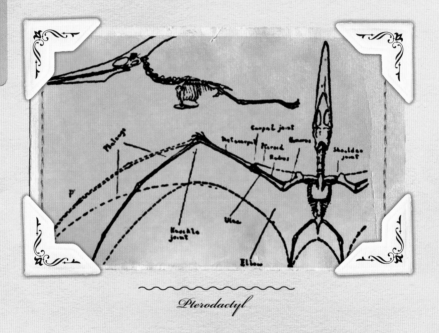

Pterodactyl

Pterodactyl (meaning "winged finger")—A flying, carnivorous reptile from the late Mesozoic Era.
Condor—The Western Hemisphere's largest flying land birds. The two species of condors include the California condor and the Andean condor.

According to a 2002 report in the Anchorage Daily News, *"A bird the size of a small airplane was recently said to be seen flying over southwest Alaska, puzzling scientists."*

Jersey Devil

The Jersey Devil hails from the most rural area in the most densely populated state (New Jersey) in America. Commonly described as having the head of a horse, the face of a collie dog, the wings of a bat, the body of a serpent, the legs of a crane, and the cloven hooves of a deer, the Jersey Devil sounds like a very strange hodgepodge. However, far from being comical, eyewitnesses say that the creature is frightening, and the strange hissing noises and piercing screams it emits strike fear into the hearts of all who hear it. Strange though this creature sounds—and it certainly doesn't resemble any known animal living or extinct—there are plenty of eyewitness accounts.

MONSTER FILE

Name: Jersey Devil

Size: Estimates vary but up to about 7 feet tall when standing erect on hind legs

Home: The Pine Barrens in southern New Jersey

Origins: See The Jersey Devil Myth (page 59)

Appearance: The creature is often described as a flying biped with hooves. It has a long neck, horse-like head and tail, wings, and hooves. Its eyes are often described as bright red and luminous.

In one of many eyewitness accounts, a husband and wife reported to the authorities that the creature was walking around outside their home. Police officers subsequently filed reports of shooting at it, but without causing it any harm. In another encounter, a Trenton County council member reported hearing a strange hissing sound outside his door late one night. When he opened the door, he found cloven hoof prints in the snow. In fact, hoof prints seem to be something of a theme in the sightings: when a German shepherd was found torn to pieces about 20 feet from where it had been chained, hoofed footprints surrounded the dog's body.

In another account, a telephone repairman was working in a remote part of Pine Barrens, near Pleasantville, when a creature fitting the description of the Jersey Devil chased him up a telephone pole. He stayed trapped atop the pole until a co-worker arrived. He too saw the creature and allegedly shot it in the wing but it escaped into the surrounding woods.

Jersey Devil

THE JERSEY DEVIL MYTH

Local legend has it that the Jersey Devil was born in the eighteenth century as the result of a curse. An English woman named Mowas Leeds had married a Pine Barren's businessman. After bearing him twelve children, she was dismayed to be pregnant with her thirteenth. She cursed the unborn child, saying, "I don't want anymore children! Let it be a devil." When the child was born, it was horribly deformed. The horrific newborn spread its wings and made its escape through the chimney into nearby woods, from where it began its reign of terror.

SECTION NOTES AND OBSERVATIONS

Creatures of Interest

_____

_____

_____

Personal Observations

_____

_____

_____

_____

_____

_____

_____

_____

Creature Photo

place picture here

MONSTERS OF CENTRAL
AND SOUTH AMERICA

"There still remains to mortify a wit,
The many-headed monster of the pit."

—English poet Alexander Pope

Central and South America have some of the most dramatic and extreme geography on the planet—and perhaps, as a consequence, some of the strangest cryptids too.

First, there's the Amazon River, the widest and second longest river in the world, running from Peru across Brazil to the Atlantic. The Amazon River Basin is also home to the largest rain forest on Earth. The basin—roughly the size of the contiguous United States—covers some 40 percent of the South American continent and includes parts of eight South American countries. One can just imagine how many unknown and as yet undiscovered animals may be roaming in this vast unexplored jungle.

Add to this the strange tales of lost Incan and Mayan civilizations from South and Central America, and remote reaches where forests have swallowed up whole cities, and you begin to realize that this continent could very well be the natural home of any number of mysterious creatures.

Chupacabra

The legend of the Chupacabra began in 1987 when Puerto Rican newspapers began reporting on a large number of gruesome deaths of farmers' livestock, including birds, boars, pigs, horses, and goats. Authorities first suspected that the killings were random, and possibly carried out by a local satanic cult. However, the slaughter spread and many farms reported a loss of livestock. The killings had one thing in common—each dead animal had two puncture holes in its neck through which blood had been drained. The creature responsible eventually was named for its vampire style of slaughter: El Chupacabra, Spanish for "goat sucker."

In Puerto Rico and Mexico, Chupacabra stories gained cult status and sightings are common, although the origins of this hybrid quasi-reptilian, porcupine-quilled, blood-sucking creature are not clear. Some reports claim that the Chupacabra's eyes have the ability to hypnotize and paralyze its prey, allowing the creature to suck the animal's blood and devour its organs.

MONSTER FILE

Name: Chupacabra

Size: Between 3 and 4 feet tall

Home: Puerto Rico and Mexico; also spotted throughout the Americas from Maine to Chile

Origins: Some believe the Chupacabra is a surviving dinosaur, others believe it is an anomalous biological entity—an escaped alien pet or experiment gone awry.

Appearance: A heavy lizard-like creature about the size of a small bear with a row of sharp spines or quills running from its neck to the base of its tail. It has a greenish-gray, leathery, scaled skin. It has a dog-like nose and face, a fork tongue, and large fangs. When it screeches, its eyes are reported to glow red. It hops in a similar fashion to a kangaroo.

Sucuriju

Native stories have always told tales of the Sucuriju, a huge, snake-like monster. When the Spaniards started to explore the tropical forests of the continent, they too returned telling stories of enormous snakes, some up to eighty feet long, which they called "matora," or "bull eater."

Name: Sucuriju

Also Known As: Giant Anaconda

Size: Between 45 and 130 feet in length

Home: The jungles of South America

Appearance: Very similar to a standard green anaconda, only bigger. It is dark brown with blackish rings and oval spots.

On January 24, 1948, *The Diario* newspaper in Brazil published a picture with the headline "Anaconda Weighing 5 Tons." It pictured a giant anaconda that had been disturbed by a group of natives after consuming a bull! The Indians measured it at 131 feet long.

Herpetologist– A snake expert

Later that year, another Brazilian newspaper, *A Noite Illustrada,* carried a photograph of an anaconda slaughtered by the militia—this one measured 115 feet. Herpetologists won't accept either photograph as evidence because there is no scale given. The photo supposedly shows the back end of a bull hanging out of the snake's mouth, but skeptics argue that it could be the hind-quarters of a small animal such as the capybara. Skeptics claim the creature is not the Sucuriju, but a standard 35-foot anaconda.

Legendary British explorer Colonel Percy Fawcett, an officer of the Royal Engineers, was sent to map parts of the Amazon between 1915 and 1925. He recorded a frightening encounter with what many believe to be the Sucuriju:

"I sprang for my rifle as the creature began to make its way up the bank and smashed a .44 bullet into its spine. At once, there was a fury of foam and several heavy thumps against the boat's keel, shaking us as though we had run on a snag. We stepped ashore and approached the creature with caution. As far as it was possible to measure, a length of 45 feet lay out of the water and 17 feet lay in the water, making it a total length of 62 feet. Its body was not thick, not more than 12 inches in diameter, but it had probably been long without food."

Percy Fawcett

Ucu

The Ucu is South America's equivalent of the Sasquatch. There have been many sightings of Bigfoot's southern cousin since the mid-twentieth century, and a particular spate of reports at the beginning of this millennium. Locals who live in these mountainous regions have long spoken of ape-men roaming the area. The earliest recorded sightings include a number of reports from local villagers in the foothills of the Andes, near Tolor Grande, Argentina in 1957; and in the Cordilleras, near Rengo, Chile, in May 1958.

MONSTER FILE

Name: Ucu

Also Known As: Ucumar or Ukumar-zupia

Size: Estimates vary from 5 to 7 feet and above

Footprints: The average footprint measures around 15.5 to 17 inches.

Home: Mountainous regions of northern Argentina and Chile

Origins: Some experts believe that the Ucu, like the Sasquatch, is a humanoid creature that has developed more slowly than the human race, but others firmly believe it is an upright walking ape related to the *Gigantopithecus*, an extinct giant ape.

Appearance: These shy creatures are covered in long hair ranging in color from black and dark brown to red and gray. They have a loping walk and can run as fast as a horse. They are able to stride over high fences.

The most recent collection of sightings, which occurred in 2003, centered on the town of Arroyo Salado in Argentina's Salta Province. One of the most extraordinary accounts collected by investigators at the time was that of Patricio Saldaño, caretaker of the local garbage dump, who, along with his wife and children, saw the Ucu at very close range.

Saldaño's dogs started barking wildly so he grabbed a torch and headed toward his pigsties. There, standing on its hindlegs was a huge hairy hominid with massive claws, waving its long arms threateningly at the dogs. His wife, eight-year-old daughter, and four-year-old granddaughter also witnessed the raid on the property, and fortunately the Ucu left empty handed.

> *The Ucu is South America's equivalent of the Sasquatch, or Big Foot.*

The Saldaños's story was backed by members of the Pereyra family who were on their way to the dump in their pickup truck, when an animal they described as "a big monkey" leapt over the bonnet of their truck, scratched the vehicle's body, and then vanished into the brush by the side of the road.

Also in 2003, Humberto Sosa and Susana Romano, two elite biathletes, were joined on a training run in Argentina by a large hairy hominid. After startling the creature while running on a trail in Cerro Termal, the Ucu then kept pace with the pair as they tried to run away. It shadowed them in the bush about 30 feet away. Perhaps it gave up when it realized they were no match for its extraordinary speed.

> *While visiting the mountainous regions of northern Argentina in 1979, anthropologist Silva Alicia Barrios was told by the local people that the Ucu often screamed at cows and chickens and liked to eat the payo plant, the inside of which is similar to a cabbage.*

El Cuero

Beneath the surface of a small glacial lake in the Chilean province of Neuquen in the southern Andes, there lives a dangerous and unidentified animal, known locally as El Cuero because it resembles a harmless animal hide floating on the water before it strikes. It has also been called the aquatic tiger because its attacks are extremely vicious; there are disturbing reports that it uses its hideous proboscis-like mouth—located in the middle of its torso—to suck blood from its victims.

For years, accounts of the El Cuero have circulated throughout the indigenous populations of Chile and Argentina. One particular tale involves a young mother who, while washing clothes at the Hua-Hum River, watched in horror as the creature surged out of the water and snatched her baby as it slept by her on the shore.

The shoreline of Lake Lacar is said to be littered with the remains of birds and animals—evidence of this amphibious creature's voracious appetite.

Name: El Cuero (meaning "cowhide")

Also Known As: El Bien Peinado (meaning "the smooth-headed one")

Size: Likened to a cowhide splayed out to dry, hence its nickname, "Hueke-Hueké"

Home: Lake Lacar, Chile

Origins: Some investigators speculate that El Cuero is distantly related to the family of South American freshwater stingrays known as the Stenohaline.

Appearance: It has a hairless head and spine, a body like a splayed cowhide, and a hideous face with two snail-like eyes on the end of reddish-brown stalks. It has a proboscis-like mouth that is located in the center of its torso, and some witnesses report that it has razor-sharp claws along the fringes of its sides.

Lake Lacar

South American mothers warn their children to stay away from lakes, afraid that the "Hueke-Hueké" (as they nicknamed the evil beast) will capture them otherwise. Descriptions of this carnivorous beast, also known as *The Leather*, have so much in common with *El Cuero*, that some investigators believe they are one and the same.

SECTION NOTES AND OBSERVATIONS

Creatures of Interest

_____

_____

_____

Personal Observations

_____

_____

_____

_____

_____

_____

_____

_____

Creature Photo

place picture here

CHAPTER THREE

MONSTERS OF EUROPE

"I admit that my own views are tinged with some romanticism, but certainly not to the extent that I would endure extreme hardship, even risk my life, to pursue a dream with no basis in reality."

—Dr. Roy Mackal, Biologist and Loch Ness Monster Investigator

Europe is small compared to other continents, but it is home to arguably the most famous cryptid of all time in the shape of the Loch Ness Monster. And Nessie, the Loch Ness Monster, has proved to be a magnet for crypto-enthusiasts from all over the world. Most people have also heard of the Kraken from Norway and possibly the Beast of Bodmin.

Obviously, as the human population grows and wilderness areas decrease, so the habitat for undiscovered animals disappears. But there still appears to be enough creatures of interest in some of the more remote corners of the world to keep cryptozoologists busy.

Loch Ness Monster

Loch Ness is the deepest lake in Britain (about 700 feet) and it lies surrounded by mountains in the Great Glen, an ancient fault that bisects the Highlands. The fault has been active for 400 million years—its last earthquake was in 1901. Stories of a monster living in the loch date back to the times of Roman Britain, and there have been numerous sightings over the centuries—and even some hazy photographic evidence.

Certainly, the Loch Ness Monster—or Nessie, as the locals fondly refer to it—is one of the world's most famous and studied cryptids. Amateur cryptozoologists have lined the shores of the lake hoping for a sighting and there have been many organized investigations.

Name: Loch Ness Monster

Also Known As: Nessie

Size: About 40 to 80 feet in length, with a girth of between 2 and 3 feet

Home: Loch Ness, Great Glen, Scotland

Origins: *Cryptoclidus* was a long-necked aquatic fish-eating reptile that became extinct 70 million years ago. Some believe that living pods may have survived through time and may still inhabit the underwater cave systems of the deepest part of the Loch.

Appearance: Dark gray in color with a smooth rounded head, a long neck, and a slightly thicker body with paddle type fins. The monster is said to move as fast as a motorboat, producing an enormous water wake. Other reports describe several humps appearing on the surface of the Loch.

In 1972, an underwater camera produced a close-up of a strange object in the lake. When experts used a special computer to sharpen the image, many believed it to be a monster's flipper. In 1987, a team of scientists searched the loch using high-tech sonar equipment in a project called Operation Deepscan. A flotilla of nineteen boats, each fitted with a sonar scanner, moved up the lake in a line. The machines picked up movements of an unidentified giant 240 feet below the surface. Mysterious clicking noises have also been recorded. Some scans showed huge objects moving in the deepest parts of the lake. What could these shapes be? They were bigger than sharks but smaller than whales. Crypto-enthusiasts claimed them as a family of Loch Ness monsters, but again, the murky waters kept the scientists from being certain.

So far, about 60 percent of the loch has been thoroughly searched by sonar—enough, skeptics would say, to prove that no monster exists. However, the steep stone sides of the loch and the wide temperature differences within make it hard to get accurate scans, so Nessie supporters still have hope.

The earliest Nessie story dates back to A.D. 565, when Christian missionary Saint Columba was making his pilgrimage through Scotland. He came across a native Pict burial on the shores of Loch Ness. On inquiring as to how the man had died, he was told that he'd fallen prey to the monster known as "Niseag," which lived in the loch. Saint Columba was furious about the bloody tales of this blatantly "satanic" creature, and he ordered one of his fellow missionaries, a young man named Lugne Mocumin, to swim across the loch to retrieve the dead man's boat. Mocumin plunged into the murky waters and his splashing stroke awoke the monster. The bystanders saw a disturbance in the middle of the lake as the beast stirred.

Upon witnessing the entire event, Saint Columba raised his hand, formed the sign of the cross and, invoking God's name, demanded that the creature retreat. Remarkably, the creature sank back beneath the loch's dark waters.

Sir Peter Scott, a member of an investigation team in the 1970s, dubbed the creature "Nessiteras rhombopteryx." Was it just a coincidence that this is an anagram for "Monster hoax by Sir Peter S?"

This event is sometimes credited as the cornerstone for converting the Scottish Picts to Christianity. It also sealed the legend of the Loch Ness Monster.

There have been quite a few fake reports of the Loch Ness Monster but a famous photograph of Nessie, taken in 1934 by Colonel Robert K. Wilson, a respectable London surgeon, was widely believed to be authentic until 1993, when it was revealed that his "monster" was a model stuck onto a toy submarine. The validity of the photograph is still debated today.

Wilson photo

Owlman

The Owlman—which, as its name suggests, appears as a man-sized owl—was seen between 1976 and 1978 in the vicinity of the English village of Mawnan. The first sighting was reported by two young sisters on April 17, 1976. June and Vicky Melling were vacationing with their family in the area when they saw a large, feathered "bird man" hovering over Mawnan Church. The sighting left the girls so scared that the family cut their trip short. Then, less than a month later, a fourteen-year-old girl named Sally Chapman and her friend who were camping in woods near the church reported hearing a hissing sound and turning to see a man/owl-like creature, with pointed ears and red eyes. The girls claimed that the creature flew up into the air, and that it had black pincer-like claws.

MONSTER FILE

Name: Owlman

Also Known As: The Cornish Owlman (as it was first sighted in Manwan, Cornwall)

Size: Between 6 and 7 feet tall

Home: Mawnan, Cornwall, England

Origins: Possibly an escaped eagle owl (Bubo bubo), a species that can grow more than 2 feet long with a wingspan of over 6 feet

Appearance: Looks like an owl, with pointed ears, clawed wings, and glowing red eyes. Silvery gray in color, it hisses and flies, revealing black pincer-like claws

Throughout the next two years, there were several more sightings and all the reports described the same appearance and general behavior of the Owlman. The most recent sighting came from a student from Chicago who, in a letter to a local newspaper in Truro, England, claimed she had witnessed a "man-bird ... with a ghastly face, a wide mouth, glowing eyes and pointed ears."

The term "Owlman" was coined by the colorful crypto-enthusiast Tony "Doc" Shiels, who investigated sightings in Cornwall and recorded many eyewitness reports.

There are striking similarities between the descriptions of the Cornish Owlman and the Mothman of West Virginia. The sightings of the Mothman spread over a couple of years and have become scarce.

Beast of Bodmin

Since the late 1980s, reports of a large cat roaming Bodmin Moor in Devon, England, have been circulating along with reports of inexplicably slain livestock. So widespread was the media reporting of these sightings in the mid-90s that, in 1995, the British government conducted an official investigation into the existence of the Beast of Bodmin (or BoB to its admirers). The study's findings concluded that there was "no verifiable evidence" of exotic felines loose in Britain, and that the mauled farm animals could have been attacked by indigenous species.

MONSTER FILE

Name: The Beast of Bodmin

Also Known As: BoB

Size: 2 to 3 feet tall; 4 to 5 feet long (excluding tail)

Home: Bodmin Moor, Devon, England

Origins: Some believe the Beast(s) of Bodmin are descendents of exotic pets released into the countryside by their owners in 1976 when the Dangerous Wild Animals Act made it expensive to keep big cats; other experts believe the animals could be a species of wildcat that became extinct in Britain over a hundred years ago. Others postulate that these cats could be relics of a native pre-ice age big cat lingering unnoticed in our countryside.

Appearance: Principally brown or black and sometimes spotted and leopard-like.

Sightings of BoB still continue and the most compelling evidence to date is a short piece of video footage that shows the black, 3½-foot-tall creature quite clearly. There's also a plaster cast of a pawprint, taken by police officers after an encounter, that is 5 inches long and 4 inches wide—one of the many fragments of "hard" evidence that supports the theory that big cats roam the wilds of Britain.

> *There are so many sightings now reported that there is a website: www.bigcatsinbritain.org dedicated to such encounters run by researcher Mark Fraser.*

It is estimated that up to 7,000 people a year see a panther-like (black) creature or a puma-like (brown) beast at large in Britain. It has become such a phenomenon that these are now known as sightings of Anomalous Big Cats (ABCs), and the number has snow-balled since the late 1980s when the Beast of Bodmin first became famous.

Although the Beast of Bodmin is the best known of Britain's feline cryptids, it has been joined over the years by the Exmoor Beast, the Fen Tiger, the Pedmore Panther, the Thing from the Ling, the Beast of Shap, the Lincolnshire Lynx, the Wildcat of the Wolds, the Beast of Roslin and many, many more unknown species.

Although the Beast of Bodmin is the best known of Britain's feline cryptids, it has been joined over the years by the Exmoor Beast, the Fen Tiger, the Pedmore Panther, the Thing from the Ling, the Beast of Shap, the Lincolnshire Lynx, the Wildcat of the Wolds, the Beast of Roslin and many, many more unknown species.

Kraken

Once thought to be the source of Norwegian legend, the many-armed Kraken is now believed to be a giant squid that still exists today.

The first people to discover evidence of the Kraken (apart from sailors who have spotted it) were the crews of nineteenth-century whaling ships. As they hauled the carcasses alongside their ships, they noted that some of the whales had scars shaped like giant suction cups on them, indicating they had survived a ferocious battle.

MONSTER FILE

Name: Kraken

Size: Approximately 50 feet in length

Home: Coasts of Norway and Iceland

Origins: Most experts now concede that the Norwegian Kraken is probably a giant squid.

Appearance: A reddish-brown gargantuan-sized octopus-like creature with countless thrashing tentacles covered in monstrous suckers.

Similarly, in the 1930s a 15,000-ton tanker was snared in the tentacles of a giant squid and during World War II, a huge squid measuring 159 feet long was sighted swimming alongside a warship.

In 1896 the remains of what appeared to be a Kraken washed up on Anastasia Island, Florida, off the coast of St. Augustine. Some of the arm fragments measured over 8 meters in length.

Yale University zoologist A. E. Verrill estimated the total arm length of the original animal may have reached 25 meters. Verrill initially supported the idea that the remains were those of a giant octopus. Later he changed his mind, suggesting the remains came from a sperm whale.

Investigators working with preserved samples subsequently confirmed the identification of a cephalopod of unknown type. In 1995, a highly disputed new analysis challenged the octopus identification, insisting that the remains came from a whale. Some believe the Anastasia Island remains came from two different animals: the arms from a Kraken, and the remainder from a sperm whale. It has been speculated that perhaps the two killed each other in mortal combat.

F. T. Bullen, author of the 1901 book, The Cruise of the Cachalot, *reported that he'd witnessed a harpooned sperm whale disgorging thousands of squid (its normal diet), and that among the debris were huge bits of tentacle as thick as a man's body.*

Kraken

In his book, A History of the Earth and Animated Nature, *Oliver Goldsmith says of the Kraken, "To believe all that has been said of the sea-serpent, or the Kraken, would be credulity; to reject the possibility of their existence would be presumption."*

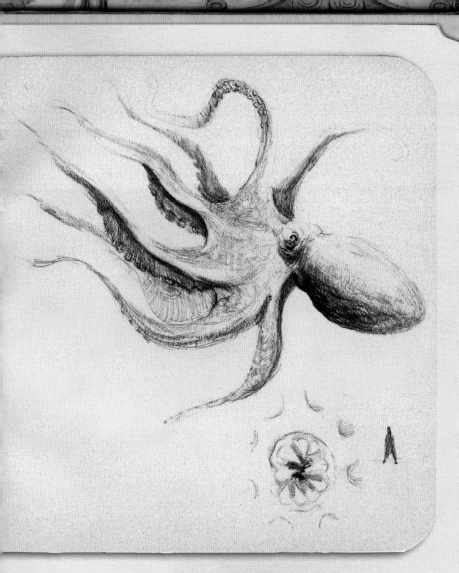

Long the muse of science fiction writers and believed to be a mythical creature, the giant squid exists and is actually the world's second largest invertebrate. In 2004, it was photographed in the wild for the first time by scientists from the National Science Museum of Japan and the Ogasawara Whale Watching Association. The specimen measured approximately 25 feet long. The same team filmed a giant squid two years later in 2006.

Tatzelwurm

Cryptozoologists are perplexed over the aquatic amphibian creature known as the Tatzelwurm of the Swiss and Austrian Alps. Should it be classified as a lake monster or sea serpent that travels across land (presumably between Alpine lakes), or is it a lizard, or perhaps a variant of a giant salamander with rather shriveled back legs, which was once native to the European Alps?

The debate may in fact be academic, since sightings of the Tatzelwurm have become so rare that some cryptozoologists believe it has become extinct during our living history.

MONSTER FILE

Name: Tatzelwurm

Size: From 1 feet up to 6 feet in length

Footprints: The average footprint measures around 15½ to 17 inches.

Home: European Alps (Austria and Switzerland)

Origins: Probably a giant lizard or salamander once native to the European Alps

Appearance: Described as a dragon-like beast. It has the features of both lizard and snake, with smooth, hairless skin covered with delicate scales. It has two small front legs. Its head is very distinctive and looks like that of a large cat, except with scales rather than fur. Its eyes are large and red.

Witness reports center on Tatzelwurm attacks on small farm animals such as chickens. The reports tend to support the argument that the creature is an evolution from a giant lizard, which is carnivorous, rather than a giant salamander, which eats only bugs and small fish.

In 1908, however, a professional hunter reported an encounter with the beast to the Austrian authorities. He said it resembled a worm 1½-feet-long and 3 inches thick, walking on four short legs. Upon the hunter's approach, the Tatzelwurm attacked him, but despite his knife swings, the blade barely penetrated the beast's leathery skin.

By the hunter's account, the creature made half a dozen attacks before retreating beneath a rock, where it declined his persistent attempts to make it come out for a photograph.

What is agreed from the sightings to date is that the Tazelwurm is scaly like a snake but has small front legs. Eyewitnesses claim that it is fearless and aggressive if surprised, but is able to conceal itself easily and hard to find when hunted. Its most distinctive feature is its feline, scaly head, which has large red eyes.

SECTION NOTES AND OBSERVATIONS

Creatures of Interest

Personal Observations

Creature Photo

place picture here

CHAPTER FOUR

MONSTERS OF AUSTRALIA

"The truth is never pure and seldom simple."

—Oscar Wilde

Some might say that the native wildlife of Australia and New Zealand is so vast that a cryptid could pass among the natural animal population unnoticed. Certainly when kangaroos, wallabies, koala bears, and duck-billed platypuses were first described in the late 1700s by explorers to the folks back home, their sightings were met with incredulity, astonishment, and a fair amount of skepticism.

Small wonder that a land that that is home to a vast and wonderful fauna has a colorful supply of cryptids too. Many of the creatures under investigation are featured in the stories of the native Aboriginal people of Australia and, in some cases, there is skeletal evidence to support the aboriginal descriptions.

The biggest problem for modern day monster hunters "down under" is that the continent is so vast, and its unsettled areas so inhospitable, that finding evidence of the potential monsters is not easy. After initial sightings, these creatures have often disappeared into the bush, swamps, or creeks and the trail goes cold.

There have been plenty of sightings nonetheless and, in 1848, settlers even captured a "Sea Kangaroo" with a long neck and

shaggy mane in a lake in Port Fairy, Victoria. Sightings of this elusive monster are still reported today.

In fact, many Australians believe that some of the cryptids discussed in this chapter are actual Australian inhabitants rather than "undiscovered" creatures. However, the perennial problem is a lack of conclusive evidence.

Bunyip

According to the Aboriginal people of Australia, Bunyips lurk in swamps, billabongs, creeks, riverbeds, and waterholes. During the night, their blood-curdling cries can be heard in the distance as they devour any animal that ventures near.

There is no photographic evidence of the Bunyip, only the eyewitness testimonies of the native Aboriginal people and verbal accounts from early settlers have documented its existence. Experience has demonstrated that, given enough time, local tales are often proven accurate. After all, the platypus was considered a hoax when first reported, but the Aboriginal people insisted on its existence from the beginning.

MONSTER FILE

Name: Bunyip

Size: 3 to 6 feet in length

Home: Australia

Origins: Possible descendant of the Diprotodon, which became extinct 50,000 years ago.

Appearance: While descriptions vary wildly, commonly cited features include a long body, a dog-like face with a horse-like tail, flippers and walrus-like tusks.

William Buckley, an escaped convict, may have been the first recorded man to spot a Bunyip. After escaping prison and going on the run, Buckley lived with Victorian Aborigines (indigenous Australians) from 1803–1835. His experiences, including his Bunyip sightings, were published in 1852. He recalls, "I could never see any part (of the Bunyip) except the back, which appeared to be covered in features of a dusky-grey color. It seemed to be about the size of a full-grown calf and sometimes larger."

The explorer Hamilton Hume lent credence to the existence of the Bunyip when, in April 1818, he discovered large bones from an unidentified creature near Lake Bathurst. Three years later, funded by The Philosophical Society of Australia, he set off to retrieve the bones for their examination, but he never returned.

Sightings continued to be reported but descriptions fell into two distinct categories, leading investigators to believe that there may be two types of bunyip—one with a dog-like appearance, and the other with a longer neck.

In 1821, the *Sydney Gazette* carried a report by an eyewitness of the Bunyip: "My attention was attracted by a creature casting up water and making a noise, in sound resembling a porpoise…. It had the appearance of a bulldog's head, but perfectly black…."

Later that same year, another eyewitness report appeared describing the beast: "Its neck was long, apparently about 3 feet out of the water, and about the thickness of a man's thigh."

In 1866, the reputation of the bunyip was so well-known in Australia it was featured on the front cover of a local version of Punch *magazine.*

In 1846, an unusual skull was found in the banks of the Murrumbidgee River in New South Wales, Australia. Several experts declared that the skull was unknown to science, leaving others to declare it the remains of a Bunyip. In 1847, the Bunyip skull was put on exhibition in the Australian Museum in Sydney for two days and it drew a huge crowd.

The skull's presence legitimized people's experiences, and many people started to speak out about their Bunyip encounters. Whether it was as a result of this mass out-pouring or not, shortly after the powers-that-be concluded that the skull was a "freak of nature" and not a new species at all. The Bunyip skull disappeared from the museum soon after and has never been seen since.

BUNYIP BLOODLINES

The hippopotamus-sized Diprotodon was the largest marsupial that ever lived. It browsed on tree leaves, shrubs, and perhaps some grasses as it wandered through the open forest, woodlands, and grasslands. Apart from the Bunyip, Diprotodon's closest living relatives are the wombats and koala.

The Diprotodon lived 1,600,000 to 40,000 years ago (during the Pleistocene epoch) and it was still living when the first people lived in Australia. Diprotodon bones have been found with butchering marks, which may have been made by early Aboriginal people using tools.

Some skeptics suggest that the Bunyip is simply a memory based on early encounters with the Diprotodon.

Masterton Monster

A large unknown creature was sighted in 1883, near the town of Masterton, New Zealand. The fearful townsfolk set their dogs upon the beast but the ferocity of the creature's attack on the first dog caused all the remaining dogs to run for their lives.

It was said to have short legs, a thick body covered in coarse, curly hair and a ferocious-looking muzzle.

The experiences at Masterton were reported in the *New Zealand Times* on May 9, 1883. The account ends there but parallels have been drawn with an Australian incident that occurred seven years later.

Similar events were reported as taking place near the town of Euroa, Australia, in the Melbourne Argus, on February 28, and again on March 1, 1890. Many witnesses testified that their village was being terrorized by "a 30-foot long, unidentifiable monstrosity," the description of which bore striking similarity to the Masterton Monster.

Soon to be dubbed the Euroa Beast, the creature brought such chaos and devastation to this small community that authorities at the Melbourne Zoological Gardens decided that the accounts deserved further scrutiny.

Zoo officials sent an emissary to Euroa armed with a "big net." Once the intrepid investigator arrived in the terrorized town, he managed to persuade forty men to accompany him on a beast hunt, in hope of capturing the creature alive. Although the men hunted day and night, the only reward they had for their labors was the discovery of a set of gigantic tracks, which petered out before the monster could be found.

MONSTER FILE

Name: Masterton Monster

Also Known As: Euroa Beast

Size: 30 feet in length

Home: Masterton, New Zealand and Euroa, Victoria, Australia

Origins: Researchers believe that this creature is probably mammalian rather than reptilian. The creature is associated by some with the ancestral amphibian known as Pederpes finneyae—a short, squat crocodile-like creature which scientists believe represents the missing link between fish and land animals.

Appearance: Broad muzzle, short legs, and thick, curly hair. Stubby, crocodile-like creature.

Yowie

Not surprisingly, Australia also has its very own hairy hominid. Sightings of the hominid date back to the 1800s, when European settlers recorded encoutering the Yowie. Sightings continue up to the present day. The descriptions match the much earlier Aboriginal traditions of the Doolagahl, or "great hairy man."

The Aboriginal people both feared and respected the Doolagahl, venerating it as a scared creature from the Dreamtime, the sacred, spiritual time during which all things take life. They describe them as terrifying to look at and fearsome.

MONSTER FILE

Name: Yowie

Also Known As: Doolagahl (meaning "great hairy man")

Size: Normally between 5 and 7 feet tall (but can be up to 14 feet tall)

Home: Primarily New South Wales, Victoria, the Gold Coast of Queensland and Tasmania, Australia

Origins: An extinct hominoid called *Meganthropus*, or possibly *Gigantopithecus*

Appearance: Yowies have an appearance similar to Bigfoot. Their entire body is covered in thick black or brown hair. They are bipedal but can run on all fours. They also give off a fowl stench when approached.

Giant fossil tracks have been found in Australia that suggest the man-like ape *Gigantopithecus* once walked the land.

These fossilized tracks closely resemble the freshly made casts of tracks made by what's believed to be the modern-day Yowie.

A recent sighting took place on September 19, 2006 when a group of four friends were on a horse riding trip in the Mega-long Valley, Blue Mountains in New South Wales. One of the women spotted a hairy ape-man creature noticed a particular stench that came from it. Her horse refused to budge until the creature moved off into the bushes. She then was able to catch up with her friends.

However, about a half hour later, the creature "just popped out from behind a bush," the woman said, startling the whole party before disappearing again. This time, the woman's horse was completely spooked and bolted up the path, throwing her against a boulder. She needed hospital attention for broken ribs and deep cuts and all were badly shocked by the encounter.

THE DEVIL MAN

As well as the Yowie, Australia has another hairy hominid known as the Yahoo. This creature walks on all fours like a bear and has dark fur on its back and sides, with lighter fur on the head, arms, legs, and belly. It's thought to be an undiscovered species of giant wombat or possibly a diprotodont, an allegedly extinct ape-like marsupial.

The confusion arises because although some cryptozoologists use the above classifications for the Yowie and the Yahoo, others differentiate between the two by claiming that the Yahoo is the "devil man" of Aboriginal legend, and the Yowie is the hairy hominid of modern sightings.

SECTION NOTES AND OBSERVATIONS

Creatures of Interest

_____

_____

_____

Personal Observations

_____

_____

_____

_____

_____

_____

_____

_____

Creature Photo

place picture here

CHAPTER FIVE

MONSTERS OF AFRICA

"We must go beyond textbooks, go out into the bypaths and untrodden depths of the wilderness and travel and explore and tell the world the glories of our journey."

—Historian John Hope Franklin

Known in the past as the "Dark Continent," Africa certainly hides its secrets well. Much of its terrain is unexplored and inaccessible, and any number of unknown monsters could still exist in its wild interior. In particular, the vast, deep swamps of East Africa, so overgrown with vines and undergrowth it makes human travel nearly impossible, are prime sites for the discovery of unknown creatures.

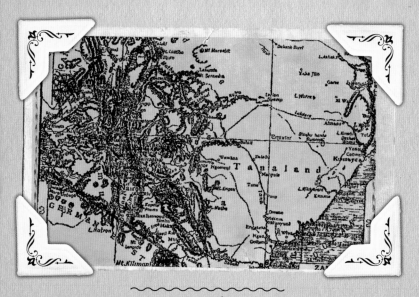

East Africa

Agogwe

Small hairy hominids known as Agogwe have been known to the local African population for centuries. The first chronicled report of the Agogwe came in the early 1900s when British big game hunter Captain William Hitchens encountered them while hunting lions in East Africa. Hitchens tried to pursue the two Agogwe into the jungle but they were too fast and the brush was too impenetrable for him to catch them. Hitchens published a report of his encounter in the London magazine *Discovery* in 1937, but without any evidence, he was publicly ridiculed.

MONSTER FILE

Name: Agogwe

Also Known As: Kakundak in Zimbabwe; Sehit in the Ivory Coast

Size: 3 to 4 feet tall

Home: The forests of East Africa, particularly Tanzania

Origins: Bernard Heuvelmans believed the Agogwe to be a surviving species of *Gracile australopithecine*, a bipedal primate from approximately 4.5 million years ago.

Appearance: A small human-like biped with long arms, long rust colored woolly hair, and a yellow-red skin under its coat. Its feet are 6 inches long with opposable toes.

As though to support Hitchens's claims, a year later eyewitness Cuthbert Burgoyne wrote a letter to the same magazine stating that he and his wife had seen something similar to

Hitchens's Agogwe while traveling along the coast of Portuguese Africa in a Japanese cargo boat in 1927. In Burgoyne's account, the couple was watching a troupe of baboons on shore through a telescope when "two little brown men" came down among the baboons to hunt. He said, "At the time, I was thrilled as they were quite evidently no beast of which I had heard or read."

A similar creature exists which locals in Mozambique call the "Agogure" or "Agogue." It is said to be just as grotesque as the Agogwe, but this tiny hominid is rumored to be more mischievous than menacing.

In recent years, there have been very few sightings of the Agogwe but this may be more a result of the ongoing wars and civil strife in the east African region rather than the disappearance of the Agogwe themselves.

Although many believe the theory that the Agogwe is a surviving species of *gracile Australopithecine*, others contest that it is more likely to be an unknown race of human pygmy. And, since the discovery of the 3-foot-species *Homo floresiensis*—dubbed the "Hobbit"—on Flores Island, east of Java, in 2004 (see page 160), more people are now giving credit to the theory that the Agogwe is also part of the *Homo genus* and perhaps yet another "hobbit" soon to join the human family tree.

When a friend and fellow big game hunter told Cuthbert Burgoyne about his own encounter with the Agogwe while on a hunting trip in Portuguese East Africa, he claimed that his native gun-bearers forbade him from shooting at the creatures—apparently a family comprising of a mother, father and child.

Kongamoto

Kongamoto means "overwhelmer of boats" in the native language of Zambia, and this terrifying reptilian flying attacker is reputed to have capsized hundreds of canoes, killing many local people in the process. It also has a reputation among the locals for causing death to anyone that looks into its eyes.

Many early explorers received verbal accounts of the Kongamoto, and, in 1942, Colonel C. R. S. Pitman was shown tracks of the creatures, with evidence of a large tail dragging along the ground. Skeptics were forced to take note when an explorer in the employment of the British Museum recounted his own Kongamoto encounter. In 1932–1933, the Percy Sladen Expedition went to West Africa under the leadership of Ivan T. Sanderson. While in the Assumbo Mountains in Cameroon, Sanderson shot a fruit-eating bat that then fell into the water. He waded in to the river to retrieve his catch but lost his balance in the fast-moving current. As he stood back up, he heard his companion on the bank shouting a warning, giving Sanderson time to bob back under the water as a huge winged creature swept down toward him. He described it "... coming straight at me only a few feet above the water was a black thing the size of an eagle. I had only a glimpse of its face, yet that was quite sufficient, for its lower jaw hung open and bore a semicircle of pointed white teeth set about their own width apart from each other." The monster flew off and Sanderson made it back to the bank where his colleague had been shooting at the creature.

The unknown bat/bird returned once more before night fell, swooping at Sanderson's colleague, causing them both to duck. The natives confirmed that it was a Kongamoto (or Olitiau in the local dialect), and then they fled, leaving all their valuables behind.

Name: Kongamoto

Also Known As: Olitiau

Size: Wingspan measures 4 to 7 feet

Home: Jiundu swamps in the Mwinilunga district of Zambia, Africa

Origins: Many scientists believe that the creature is a living pterodactyl.

Appearance: Consistently described as a massive ugly bat-like monster. It has no feathers, but instead has a smooth black or red skin, and it possesses a beak full of sharp razor-like teeth.

Although Sanderson, as a respected zoologist, has probably been the most credible authority to see a Kongamoto, sightings have since continued.

In 1988, Professor Roy Mackal led an expedition to Africa to investigate reports of a giant flying lizard with a wingspan of up to 30 feet. Reports suggested that this cryptid usually glided but was capable of true flight. Although the expedition was unsuccessful in terms of providing hard evidence, one team member, James Kosi, reported seeing the creature from about 1,000 feet away. He described it as "a giant glider shape, black with white markings."

Pterosaurs were carnivorous flying reptiles that thrived and became extinct at the same time as the dinosaurs. These terrifying beasts are said to have died out over 60 million years ago, but reports of sightings of pterodactyl-like creatures have been made all over the world in the last 200 years, most frequently in Africa, leading to speculation that the Kongamoto may be a living pterosaur.

In 1923, Frank H. Melland was traveling in Zambia where he started collecting native reports of ferocious flying reptiles. When local inhabitants were shown drawings of various animals, including a pterosaur, each one immediately and unhesitatingly identified the pterosaur as the Kongamoto.

Mokèlé-mbèmbé

Mokèlé-mbèmbé, which translates as "one who stops the flow of rivers," is the central African equivalent of the Loch Ness Monster. It is reputed to inhabit the Likouala swamps and Lake Tele in the Congo—a remote and inaccessible area that is days from civilization by road.

Apart from native sightings, the first European report of the beast appeared in a 1776 history for French missionaries. Then, in 1903, Captain von Stein zu Lausnitz led an expedition to the Likouala area. He heard local reports that the creature was as big as an elephant with a long muscular tail and that, although it was an herbivore, it would attack and kill humans and hippopotami and was extremely territorial. Sadly, the team left the area empty handed.

MONSTER FILE

Name: Mokèlé-mbèmbé (meaning "one who stops the flow of rivers")

Size: Around 15 to 30 feet in length

Home: Likouala swamps and Lake Tele in the Congo, Central Africa, in particular clay caves located on the sharp bends of rivers.

Origins: Many believe it is a relict sauropod (dinosaur), which somehow survived extinction.

Appearance: A beast larger than an African elephant with enormous footprints. It has a long flexible neck and a muscular tail like that of an alligator. It has smooth brownish–gray skin like that of an elephant and some researches describe it as having only one long and prominent tooth.

In 1980, renowned cryptozoologist Roy Mackal, with herpetologist James H. Powell, led an expedition deep into the swamps of Likouala country in search of the Mokèlé-mbèmbé. They met many of the eyewitnesses who eagerly identified a sauropod dinosaur from books as the creature they had seen.

The director of the Wildlife and Protected Areas in the Republic of Congo, Dr. Marcellin Agnagna—a respected zoologist from the Brazzaville University—reports that he had a twenty-minute eyewitness experience with the Mokèlé-mbèmbé at Lake Tele in April 1983, and he recorded the whole encounter. Unfortunately, he left the lens cap on the camera.

While the 2001 crypto-safari team was in Cameroon, there was a distinct lack of hippopotami or crocodiles in their search area, even though this was their perfect natural habitat and these creatures used to thrive there. Locals attribute the absence of crocs and hippos to the presence of the Mokèlé-mbèmbé in the vicinity.

The most recent sighting was made at the turn of the millennium when two security guards at a ferry station in Cameroon were terrified by the approach of a huge long-necked creature as it swam down the river in the rainy season. Given the depth of the swollen river, they reckoned its neck must have been at least 12 feet in length. The men deserted their post and fled.

A local fisherman told monster hunters that a Mokèlé-mbèmbé had been killed in 1959 by a band of pygmies. Apparently, all those who ate its meat subsequently died.

In recent years, the Likouala and Lake Tele regions have become too unstable for monster investigators to visit. When a Mokèlé-mbèmbé look alike was reported in Cameroon, a team of experts set off in February 2001 to investigate. During their trip, they met and interviewed several eyewitnesses including a Bantu boy who described a huge creature with a long neck, massive body, and bad temper if disturbed.

The investigators also ran a controlled experiment. They showed local villagers and witnesses a book of wild animals. The locals could identify African animals but were mystified by pictures of native North American animals. Remarkably though, all could pick out the Mokèlé-mbèmbé from the book—they were actually pointing to illustrations of brachiosaurs and diplodocuses, which are dinosaurs that became extinct 65 million years ago.

Dingonek

The Dingonek is another lake monster from the Congo, which is sometimes confused with the Mokèlé-mbèmbé, even though its reported features bear no resemblance to its more famous relative.

In contrast to the Mokèlé-mbèmbé, the Dingonek is 12 feet in length, with a squarish head and a long horn, saber-like canines, and a tail complete with a bony, dart-like appendage that secretes a deadly poison. This mysterious cryptid is covered in a scaly, mottled epidermis, which has been likened to the prehistoric-looking anteater known as the pangolin (something like a flexible thin-skinned tortoise).

The first reported sighting of a Dingonek was around 1909. The account of the sighting was recorded in Edgar Beecher Bronson's book Closed Territory, which details the experiences of his friend, a hunter and adventurer. While traveling along the banks of the Gori river in Western Africa, the hunter came across a Dingonek, which he described as "a terrifying animal." The description he gave matched that of the Dingonek—it described the creature's footprints that he saw on the muddy banks as like those of a hippopotamus but with claws. Like the Mokèlé-mbèmbé, the Dingonek has been known to kill crocodiles, hippopotami, and even humans.

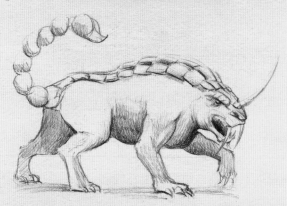

Name: Dingonek

Size: Around 12 feet in length

Home: Lakes and swamps of the Congo (especially in area formally known as Zaire)

Origins: Unknown

Appearance: The Dongonek is covered in scales and resembles a large pangolin. Its bulky body is covered in leopard-like spots and its feet have reptilian claws. It has a blockish head with a long horn on its forehead and two saber-like canines. It also has a bony tail with a poisonous dart, rather like a sting-ray.

In 1913, the German government sent an exploratory expedition, led by Captain von Stein zu Lausnitz, to the Cameroon to search for undiscovered animals. The team returned with many local accounts of Dingonek sightings and reports of how the creature would attack canoes that ventured too close, but the expedition was prematurely terminated due to the start of World War I before the team could secure their own documentary evidence.

SECTION NOTES AND OBSERVATIONS

Creatures of Interest

_____

_____

_____

Personal Observations

_____

_____

_____

_____

_____

_____

_____

_____

Creature Photo

place picture here

CHAPTER SIX

MONSTERS OF ASIA

"It is not the critic who counts, not the man who points out how the strong man stumbled, or where the doer of deeds could have done better. The credit belongs to the man who is actually in the arena."

—Theodore Roosevelt

Asia and its territories have some of the world's truly unexplored terrain, including the impenetrable forests of Borneo.

Given that known species can hide from investigators in these environments without detection for years—the shy and elusive Borneo rhino was only caught on video for the first time recently—it stands to reason that unknown creatures could remain undiscovered with ease.

However, there are plenty of local stories about many creatures and these tales are enough to whet the appetite of keen crypto-enthusiasts across the globe.

Yeti

Long before Western mountaineers began to explore the Himalayas, local people had many stories and sightings of the Yeti—sometimes referred to as the Abominable Snowman of the Himalayas—roaming the icy mountain passes.

The earliest recorded Western sighting was in 1832 by a British diplomat at the Nepalese court; B. H. Hodgson wrote that some local people who were with him on a hunting trip became frightened by a "wild man" covered in long dark hair.

Some fifty years later, explorer Major L. A. Waddell discovered Yeti footprints in the snow, and in 1925, N. A. Tomabazi, a Fellow from the Royal Geographical Society in London, saw a Yeti on the Zemu Glacier. It vanished before he could take a photo.

Since those early reports, hundreds of people have studied the mystery of the Yeti, and still the sightings of these and other similar creatures keep rolling in.

The Sherpas of the High Himalayas fear and respect Yetis, viewing them as an evil force—they believe that crossing a Yeti's path will bring bad luck, illness, or even death.

So, once a year, they hold a festival to drive evil spirits out of their villages. One man wears a sacred headdress of skin and hair and he represents the spirit of the Yeti (which they believe is sent by the gods to punish people for their misdeeds). During the ceremony, the Yeti is driven out of the village and evil is banished.

Name: Yeti (from the Sherpa words yeh the, meaning "that thing")

Also Known As: The Abominable Snowman (a mistranslation of the local word metoh-kangmi, meaning "filthy snowman")

Size: Between 7 and 8 feet tall and weighs upwards of 800 pounds (crypto-purists insist there are three forms of Yeti—a little Yeti (Teh-lma) of the mountain valleys; the man-sized Yeti (Met-teh) that sometimes tracks across snowfields, but lives mostly in the lower rain forests; and the Chemo, the giant bear, that lives higher up.)

Home: The Himalayan mountain region of Nepal and Tibet

Origins: Some experts believe the Yeti may be a descendent of the *Gigantopithecus*, the extinct giant ape. In the 1980s, anthropologists Myra Shackley and Boris Prochnev suggested the Yeti was descended from Neanderthal man, driven to the remote Himalayas by the arrival of our direct ancestors, Cro-Magnon man.

Appearance: A tall man-ape creature covered with gray shaggy monkey-like hair. It has a conical scalp, pointed ears, a hairless chest area and a human-like face. It is reported to move in an ape-like fashion and its footprints represent those of a very large human.

YETI ATTACK

In 1974, a fourteen-year-old local girl named Lhakpa Dolma was tending her herd of yaks—long-haired bovines from South Central Asia—on the mountainside when she heard a strange sound. Minutes later, she was grabbed by a huge two-legged creature that picked her up and then dumped her in a mountain stream.

She was found by her brothers, shaken and crying. Luckily for Lhakpa, the beast had abandoned her in favor of her yaks: several had been attacked and killed and the teeth marks were unlike any made by the usual predators such as wolves or snow leopards. The investigating police also noted that there were a large number of Yeti footprints at the scene—but the Yeti had gone.

Accounts by Western mountaineers of brushes with Yetis triggered a fascination in the media with these elusive beasts and even caught the attention of scientists. In fact, many expeditions have been conducted to find evidence of the hairy creature but, to date, only footprints have been found. Here are some of the highlights of recent Yeti-hunts and sightings:

✖ **1951**—Famous mountaineer Eric Shipton photographed a line of large unknown footprints in the snow. He placed his 13-inch ice ax next to a footprint to give an idea of scale (it was roughly the same size).

✖ **1960**—World Encyclopedia Scientific Expedition spent six months searching for the Yeti, to no avail.

✖ **1970**—Top British mountaineer Don Whillans saw a Yeti in the light of the moon. He watched it for ten minutes or so.

✖ **1986**—The creature was observed by the famous climber Reinhold Messner.

✖ **1988**—Canadian climber Robert Hutchison organized the Yeti Research Project. After five months, he had collected many photos of Yeti tracks but none of the creature itself.

✖ **1992**—Julian Freeman-Atwood found footprints on a glacier that no one had climbed for thirty years.

Footprints made in snow may appear bigger than they really are due to the snow melting and refreezing, thus distorting the print's shape and size. This is known in scientific circles as the freeze-thaw phenomenon, and scientists believe this accounts for the large Yeti footprints witnessed by so many mountaineers and locals.

In 2001, a long strand of black hair, believed to be from a Yeti, was found snagged on a tree in the Himalayan kingdom of Bhutan. The hair was sent for DNA testing in the U.K.

Amazingly, after analysis, Dr. Bryan Sykes of Oxford University told the press that the DNA found in the hair did not belong to any known creature. He said, "It's not human, and not anything else we have so far been able to identify. We don't know what it is." Could this be the first incontrovertible evidence that a cryptid, possibly the Yeti, does exist in the Himalayas?

Heavenly Lake Monster

The Heavenly Lake Monster lives in a remote, glacier-filled volcanic crater 6,000 feet above sea level with the icy waters that are up to 1,200 feet deep in places. The creature is said to resemble a large horse and eyewitnesses say that it "leaps repeatedly from the water in a seal-like fashion."

First sighted in 1968 by a high-ranking Chinese government official, the creature soon gained considerable notoriety. Chou Fon Yin, a member of staff in the Jilin Province Weather Department said of his experience with the creature: "I was looking at the lake and suddenly a wave emerged from the northeastern side followed by two black points. I used 6x binoculars to look at it. Oh my God! The head was just like a dog with a black-gray color. The two black points were moving under and sticking out of the water. The water wake behind the monster was at least several meters, showing that the monster swims really fast. My eyes were clear; I could not have been mistaken."

MONSTER FILE

Name: Heavenly Lake Monster

Also Known As: Chinese Nessie

Size: 30 feet in length

Home: Lake Chang bai shan Tianchi, Jilin Province, China (known to locals as the Heavenly Lake)

Origins: Possibly a surviving plesiosaur which inhabits the deep depths and the glacially formed cave systems of this huge volcanic lake

Appearance: Grayish-blackish green, with a prominent horse-like head and two small horns. Though some reports indicate more reptilian features, its body is consistently described as being covered with heavy scales.

TOURIST ATTRACTION

Hundreds of tourists have reported sightings of this creature, but in July 1994, a group of over forty Japanese tourists all claim to have watched and photographed the beast as it frolicked on the surface of the lake.

In 2005, the China Daily *newspaper reported that a fifty-two-year-old man, Zheng Changchun, had watched a strange animal in the water and had recorded the incident. No scientific response to the videotape has been forthcoming as yet.*

The press drew inevitable comparisons to the Loch Ness Monster, earning it the nickname, the Chinese Nessie. In fact, descriptions of the beast suggest it is more like the Australian Bunyip. Despite skepticism in the scientific world, the Heavenly Lake Monster seems unabashed and makes regular appearances for boatloads of visitors to the lake.

Dragon Boat Festivals started approximately 2,500 years ago in southern China along the banks of the Yangtze River and were originally carried out to please the Asian water dragon deity. Some believe that the lake monsters, particularly those that resemble horses such as the Heavenly Lake Monster, represent the water dragon deity. The rituals often included human sacrifices and violent battles between crew members of competing boats, who hurled stones and struck opponents with bamboo sticks. It was considered to be unlucky if there wasn't at least one drowning during the course of the event.

Mongolian Death Worm

Many experts believe that sightings of the Mongolian Death Worm are just legendary and purely a hoax, but local tribes (and some cryptozoologists, of course) are convinced of its existence and only recount sightings with great reluctance because they are terrified of the creature.

Descriptions of this elusive but deadly creature say that it varies in length from 2 to 5 feet and its head and tail resemble each other (some snakes use this ploy to confuse predators). It usually lives below ground, surfacing to hunt only in the rainy season (only two months of the year in this arid region). It moves in a strange rolling, wriggling manner but rises up to kill its prey by spitting venom or emitting an electric shock. It is reported to be able to kill a camel or a horse with ease and to be attracted by the color yellow. Locals tell investigators that the Death Worm can produce a venom that is lethal on contact and that the creature has the ability to kill at a distance, using an electric shock.

Czech explorer Ivan Mackerle is the undisputed expert of the Death Worm. He has mounted two expeditions in search of the creature in 1990 and 1992, and is planning a third trip, this time using an ultra-light aircraft, from which he hopes to spot the creature basking on the desert sand.

In 2005, the Centre for Fortean Zoology, along with E-Mongol (a French travel website) joined forces to mount an expedition to investigate a sighting of the creature. Although they could not find any proof that the Mongolian Death Worm exists, they concluded that it is possible for such a creature to survive undisturbed in the deep Gobi Desert along the prohibited areas of the Mongolian/Chinese border.

MONSTER FILE

Name: Mongolian Death Worm

Also Known As: Allghoi Khorkhoi (meaning "blood filled intestine worm"; it apparently looks like the intestines of a cow)

Size: Up to 5 feet in length with a 1-foot girth

Home: Sand dunes of the Gobi Desert, Mongolia

Origins: Some believe the worm is probably a reptile such as an unusual snake or a skink. It's possible the creature is a worm since there are some varieties of worms in Australia that are known to grow up to 10 feet in length.

Appearance: A fat, bright red worm that spews a yellow poison. It's hard to identify its head because the ends of this worm look much the same.

Gobi Desert

Ahool

The Sudanese people of western Java tell stories of a giant bat that has a piercing triple cry, "Ahool, ahool, ahool," from which it gets its name. There are plenty who claim to have seen the Ahool but even more who have heard its distinctive cry.

This eerie beast has the head of a monkey on a furry body that is about 2½ feet long. It has vast clawed wings that can fold back as it swoops down and skims the surface of the water. Ahools are nocturnal creatures, living in caves behind waterfalls by day and hunting for fish at night.

Currently, the largest bat recognized by mainstream science is the Bismarck flying fox, which has a wingspan of six feet at most. These large bats reside in New Guinea, uncannily close to the Java island home of the Ahool.

Name: Ahool

Size: Wingspan of nearly 12 feet

Home: Rain forests of Java, Indonesia

Origins: One theory put forward by celebrated cryptozoologist Ivan T. Sanderson is that the Ahool may belong to the giant bat suborder, Microchiroptrea, and is a relative of the Kongamoto found in northwest Zambia, Africa (see page 127).

Appearance: It has gray fur, a monkey-like head with large dark eyes, and its body is about the size of a one-year-old child. It has large claws located on the top of its forearms so it can catch fish as it skims the water with its wings folded back.

Eminent naturalist Ernest Bartels had two encounters with an Ahool. In 1925, he saw one by a waterfall near the Salek Mountains and, in 1927, he heard its readily recognizable triple cry. After his first-hand experiences, he dedicated much of his time to collecting other eyewitness accounts and to trying to prove the existence of the Ahool to a doubtful scientific community.

Buru

The gigantic Komodo dragon-like reptiles known as Buru were said to have lived in the dense, marshy lakes found deep within a remote Himalayan valley of Apa Tani, until they were hunted to extinction in the 1940s. The Dafla and Apa Tani tribes who live in the area report that the Buru was known in their isolated valley until the middle of the last century when the local tribes drained and cultivated the swamps for farmland.

Some believe the Buru is lost forever, but others are hopeful that it has been forced into even more remote areas of the Apa Tani or Rilo swamps where it still lives in small, isolated pockets.

MONSTER FILE

Name: Buru

Size: Between 12 to 15 feet long

Home: Apa Tani Valley, Himalayas, Northeast India

Origins: Perhaps a species of monitor lizard or possibly a variant crocodile

Appearance: A giant dragon-like reptile with a scaleless bluish-gray skin. It has three rows of short, blunt spines running down its back. Its head is long and elongates into a big snout that is flattened at the tip and has large tiger-like teeth. Even though it has stumpy short legs about a foot long, and heavily clawed feet, it apparently moves extremely fast. Its distinguishing feature is its tail, which is described as being 5 feet in length and covered with armored plates.

Behavior: The Buru is aquatic but raises its head from the water to make loud bellowing sounds. It has been seen nosing about in the muddy banks of rivers and swamps. It can be aggressive if provoked but prefers to keep to itself.

SWAMP HUNTERS

Ralph Izzard, a London Daily Mail *newspaper correspondent on assignment in Delhi, became captivated by tales of the Buru and was instrumental in forming an expedition to the Apa Tani and Rilo Valley in 1948 to find the creature. The team came back empty-handed.*

Charles Stonor, a firm believer in the existence of the Buru, was an English zoologist who was the first Westerner to visit the Apa Tani Valley in 1948. He is still considered the foremost expert on the isolated community and its people, legends, and flora and fauna—including the mysterious Buru.

Himalayas

Asiatic Wild Men

They may go by different names and come in various shapes and sizes, but Asia has a remarkable number of reported sightings of wild men roaming its forests and mountains.

From the huge, shaggy, human-like beast of Mongolia to the wee "ape-man" of Sumatra, Asia appears to be a hominid haven for cryptozoologists. What's more, there's now scientific evidence that at least one of these creatures, the Ebu Gogo, existed—it even has a scientific name: *Homo floriensis*.

Anthropologists have not stopped squabbling since *Homo floresiensis* was discovered. Some believe the Hobbit is a new human species, while others believe it is a skeleton of a deformed, prehistoric *Homo sapien*.

Given this latest find, who's to say that there may not still be populations of "wild men" surviving in remote parts of Asia today.

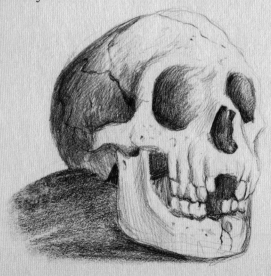

Ebu Gogo

MONSTER FILE

Name: Ebu Gogo (meaning "grandmother of he who eats anything")

Size: About 3 feet tall

Home: Island of Flores, Indonesia

Origins: The discovery in 2003 on Flores of the remains of a 3½-foot-tall humanoid, *Homo floresiensis*, suggests a human race existed on the island until at least 12,000 years ago.

Appearance: The Ebu Gobo are pot-bellied little people with prominent ears, covered in grayish hair. They have an awkward, sloping walk and are often said to murmur in what is assumed to be their own language. The women have extremely pendulous breasts.

Islanders recall stories of how the Ebu Gogo could immediately repeat what was said to them in parrot-like fashion irrespective of the length of the conversation.

Although scientists rationalize that local legends of "little people" probably represent a folk memory of the island's previous inhabitants *(Homo floresiensis)*, local villagers maintain that Ebu Gogo raided their crops and lived in local caves right up until the Dutch colonists settled the area in the nineteenth and early twentieth centuries. And they don't rule out the possibility that the Ebu Gogo may still exist in more isolated pockets of the rain forest on the island.

According to village elders, the Ebu Gogo were allowed to live side by side with the islanders until they stole—and ate—a baby from the village. They were then chased from the caves nearby and were last seen heading in the direction of Liang Bua, where the Homo floresiensis was found.

Yeren

There have been nearly 400 sightings of the Yeren since the 1920s. In 1977, the Chinese Academy of Sciences sent an expedition to find the "wild man." From the evidence that they collected—casts of footprints, samples of hair, droppings, and numerous eyewitness accounts—they concluded that the "wild man" is an unknown species of primate, and quite possibly, a descendant of *Gigantopithecus*.

MONSTER FILE

Name: Yeren (Chinese Wild Man)

Also Known As: Ranges from 5 to 7 feet tall

Size: 30 feet in length

Home: The mountains and forests of the remote Hubei Province, China

Origins: Most researchers believe this undiscovered humanoid is a direct descendent of the extinct giant ape *Gigantopithecus*, which did formerly inhabit the same region. Many of the local caves contain fossilized bones of the *Gigantopithecus*, which lends credible support to this theory.

Appearance: Covered in reddish-brown hair, the Yeren has a sloping forehead that rises above deep-set round black eyes. It has protruding lips, horse-like teeth, and a large bulbous nose with upturned nostrils. Its arms hang down below its knees. The creature has large hands, about 8 inches long, and walks awkwardly with its legs wide apart.

Wild man investigator Yuan Zhenxin believes that between 1,000 and 2,000 of the ape-like creatures roam the forests of central China, particularly the Shennongjia Nature Reserve in Hubei Province.

Baramanu

B etween 1992 and 1994, Spanish zoologist Jordi Magraner, along with Dr. Anne Mallasseand, sought evidence of the Barmanu during a trek through the Shishi Kuh Valley, where they found primate-like footprints and chronicled abundant eyewitness accounts. The European team also heard guttural sounds, which could only have been made by a primitive primate.

MONSTER FILE

Name: Barmanu (meaning "the big hairy one")

Size: Reported as being up to 7 feet tall

Home: The mountain and valley region of Shishi Kuh, Northern Pakistan

Origins: Some believe that the Barmanu could be a surviving race descended from Neanderthal man; others suggest it's a race of undiscovered wild men untouched by civilization.

Appearance: It has an appearance similar to the Neanderthal, beetle-browed and broad nosed. It has been reported to emit a distinctive guttural sound which is consistent with that produced by a primitive primate.

WHAT'S THAT SMELL?

Isolated sightings have been made by the shepherds of the Shishi Kuh who call this creature "the big hairy one." They also report that it gives off a horrific stench, causing some experts to liken it to the American Skunk-Ape (see Sasquatch, page 22).

Second Edition

Alma

There have been numerous sightings of Almas in locales ranging from the Caucuses in the west to Mongolia in the north. Many reports are from native peoples, but there have been enough Alma encounters by Western explorers, adventurers, and scientists to support claims of their existence.

British anthropologist Myra Shackley has collected numerous eyewitness accounts during her investigations of the Almas. Here is just one testimony that she recounts:

"In 1980, a worker at an experimental agricultural station, operated by the Mongolian Academy of Sciences at Bulgan, encountered the dead body of a wild man: 'I approached and saw a hairy corpse of a robust humanlike creature dried and half-buried by sand. I had never seen such a humanlike being before covered by camel-color brownish-yellow short hairs and I recoiled, although in my native land in Sinkiang I had seen many dead men killed in battle. ... The dead thing was not a bear or ape and at the same time it was not a man like Mongol or Kazakh or Chinese and Russian. The hairs of its head were longer than on its body.' "

PRISONER OF WAR

During World War II, a unit of Russian soldiers captured an Alma. It was examined but escaped. Later the Alma was recaptured, court-martialed, and executed as a deserter.

Name: Alma (Mongolian for "wild man")

Also Known As: Almasti

Size: Between 5 and 7 feet tall

Home: Central Asia (China and Mongolia)

Origins: Cryptozoologists believe Almas are either a relict population of Neanderthal or that they are simply wild men who remain untouched by human civilization.

Appearance: These human-like bipeds are covered with reddish-brown, or occasionally black, hair (often curly), and have a pronounced brow ridge, flat nose, and large jaws.

Orang-pendek

Western sightings have been reported since the early 1920s and, of all the hairy hominids mentioned in this book, scientists agree that the Orang-pendek is the most likely candidate for acceptance as a living species of human.

One member of a team of scientists who set out to discover the Orang-pendek in 1993 (funded by conservation organization Flora and Fauna International) had a startling encounter when something stepped out on to a path in front of her. She and the rest of the team concluded that the unknown creature exists and is probably a subspecies of orangutan.

MINI HOOLIGANS

Local Kubu tribes claim that unless they left tobacco for the Orang-pendek at night, these little "wild men" would go on a rampage, screeching, and yelling, until they'd destroyed the tribe's camp.

Monster File *Orang-pendek*

Name: Orang-pendek (meaning "short man")

Also Known As: Gugu, Sedapa, Sedabo, and Atu

Size: About 4 feet tall

Home: The dense rain forests of Sumatra

Origins: Some experts believe the Orang-pendek is some kind of ground-dwelling, walking orangutan variant, while others favor the idea that it is a late-surviving primitive human. Some believe that Orang-pendek is the same species as the Ebu Gogo.

Appearance: A bipedal ape-man covered in reddish fur. Although short, it is broad-shouldered and deep-chested with dainty feet. Orang-pendek is described as graceful, agile, and even attractive.

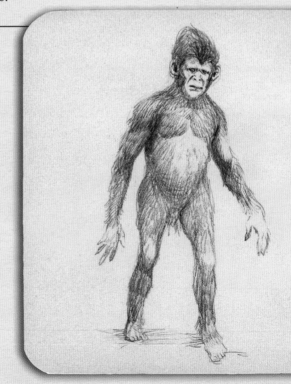

SECTION NOTES AND OBSERVATIONS

Creatures of Interest

_____

_____

_____

Personal Observations

_____

_____

_____

_____

_____

_____

_____

_____

Creature Photo

place picture here

EPILOGUE

"All things being equal, the simplest solution tends to be the best one."
—William of Ockham
Fourteenth-century English logician and Franciscan friar

In recent years, cryptozoology has received a much-needed boost in the form of a series of well-publicized scientific discoveries of hitherto unknown creatures. Surely these finds lend credence to the cryptozoology theory that there are still undiscovered animals yet to be found on this Earth? And who's to say that the Yeti, Loch Ness Monster, or Bigfoot will not be the next "unknown" creature to reveal itself.

The existence of *Homo floriensis* and the Sumatran clouded leopard, not to mention the Borneo red carnivore and the three new species of large cattle-type animals found in Vietnam, have each had their own persuasive impact on a largely doubtful scientific community.

Yet, it is probably fair to say that, until there is clear video footage of a hairy hominid or tangible physical evidence of a lake monster in the form of a carcass, cryptozoology's detractors will continue to scoff.

Nonetheless, the great thing about cryptozoologists is that, despite accusations of naivety and credulity, and occasionally, cases of open derision from their scientific peers, such charges only serve to make this intrepid band of investigators more determined to prove their critics wrong.

Cryptozoologists remain open-minded and scientifically rigorous—fervent in the belief that one day, their doggedness and hard efforts will be rewarded by the discovery of their cryptid quarry.

The burden of proof may still rest on the shoulders of the cryptozoologist, but it's worth bearing in mind the fourteenth century wisdom of William of Ockham. Philosophers, scientists, and intellects routinely work from the premise that the simplest explanation is probably the correct one, so why, when numerous eye-witnesses say they saw a creature that looked like a living dinosaur, do we dismiss the possibility that there is a living dinosaur still walking the earth?

Undoubtedly, the debate will continue to rage until evidence is found to silence the critics. In the meantime, cryptozoologists all over the world will tirelessly continue to investigate these amazing unknown creatures and, with new finds turning up each year, there's no reason to give up hope that another big discovery is not just around the corner.

Australian illustration of a Bunyip

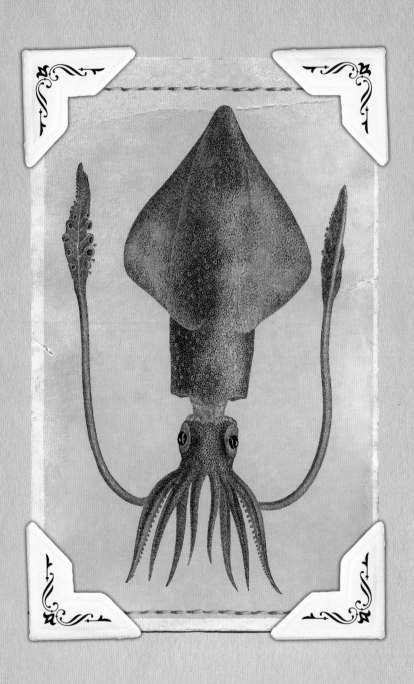

FAMOUS MONSTER HUNTERS

"He who asks a question may be a fool for five minutes. But he who never asks a question remains a fool forever."
—Tom J. Connelly

Like most people who take the road less traveled, crypto-zoologists are often unsung heroes. However, there are some great and illustrious characters throughout history that have dedicated themselves to bringing unknown animals to light.

Ancient Heroes
Herodotus (484-425 B.C.)
Known as the "Father of History," Herodotus was a Greek historian and naturalist who chronicled the wars, current affairs and natural history of his day. Some modern-day critics accuse Herodotus of mixing myth and reality when it comes to the fauna of ancient Greece, Persia, Babylon, Asia Minor, and Egypt. Others believe that Herodotus depicted animals that he personally encountered on his travels or which he believed to exist—animals that today we would recognize as cryptids.

Lucretius (c. 99-55 B.C.)
This lauded Roman poet, philosopher, and naturalist wrote many books, the most famous of which was his philosophical tome *De Rerum Natura (On the Nature of the Universe)* which combines a scientific and philosophical treatise in the form

of a poem. Lucretius explains his views on the mechanical laws of nature, the physical origins of the universe, and the atomic structure of matter.

Herodotus

Alongside his scientific view of the world, he also chronicles the animals of the day using what might be classed as modern scientific methods, and his theories on the evolution of life have made a great contribution not only to contemporary zoology but also to cryptozoology.

Olaus Magnus (1490-1558)

This pioneering Swede was fascinated by natural history and he wrote several volumes about the geography and fauna of his native Sweden. But it's his fascination with sea serpents of the north Atlantic that earns him his place in our honor roll.

Despite dismissing other "mythical" beasts out of hand, Magnus described sea serpents in a down-to-earth, scientific fashion, and his writings were so detailed and comprehensive that they inspired another Scandinavian, Erik Pontoppidan (see page 184), to take up the torch in the following century and to become the next in a long line of great north Atlantic sea serpent investigators.

Conrad Gessner (1516-1565)

Hailed as the most advanced naturalist of his era, Gessner is now known as the "Father of Zoology" in particular for his illustrated book *Historiae Animalium*, which became the standard zoological reference work throughout Europe during the sixteenth and seventeenth centuries.

Before succumbing to the plague in 1565, Gessner maintained a vast correspondence with the scholars and naturalists of the day, in which he made clear his firm belief in the existence of sea monsters.

Gessner

On August 24, 79 A.D., Pliny the Elder, against
the wishes of his wife and his followers, boarded
a boat to go and investigate the strange cloud
rising from the top of Mount Vesuvius across the
bay from his home. He perished in the volcano's
noxious fumes in pursuit of his life's passion—
natural history. In his numerous books, he de-
scribes animals that we would recognize today
and some that could most definitely be classed as
cryptids. For example, his description of "creatures living in the Land of the Satyrs, that are
swift and able to run on 2 and 4 feet. They had
human-like bodies and because of their swiftness,
can only be caught when they are ill or old" is
often interpreted as the Yeti.

Erik Ludvigsen Pontoppidan (1698-1764)

A bishop and a university professor of theology, as well as one of the most renowned chroniclers of the north Atlantic sea serpents (inspired by Olaus Magnus). He fastidiously traveled the fjords of the Norwegian coastline, collecting data and eyewitness accounts. He was rewarded with his own sighting of the extraordinary marine monsters known as the Kraken that he did so much to prove existed.

Pontoppidan

Antoon Oudemans (1858-1943)

In 1892, Dutch-born zoologist Oudemans risked his career and his considerable reputation when he published the first paper ever to deal exclusively with a cryptozoological creature, the sea serpent. He chronicled countless eyewitness reports and finally concluded that sea serpents were not giant sea snakes, nor descendants of plesiosaurs (swimming dinosaurs), but were related to mammals. He dubbed them Megophias megophias.

In the 1930s, Oudemans was the most prominent scientist to investigate the Loch Ness Monster phenomenon.

Twentieth-Century Pioneers
Ivan T. Sanderson (1911-1973)

In his youth, Sanderson, a Scot, was an explorer who mounted expeditions into some of the world's most isolated jungles, recording numerous thus-far unknown creatures—most notably, the gigantic bat-like creature known as the Olitiau, which attacked his party while he was exploring in the Assumbo Mountains of Cameroon.

In the 1950s, Sanderson gained international fame as an author and talk-show guest, discussing his theories on cryptids. His 1961 book, *Abominable Snowmen: Legend Come to Life*, became the seminal tome on the Yeti.

Bernard Heuvelmans (1916-2001)

Known as "the Father of Cryptozoology," Heuvelmans earned a doctorate in zoology from the Free University of Brussels. When World War II broke out, he was living and studying in Belgium. After escaping from the occupying Germans, Heuvelmans eventually managed to eke out a living as a jazz performer until 1948 when he read an article by Ivan T. Sanderson that inspired him to devote the rest of his life to the search for "hidden animals."

In 1955, Heuvelmans published one of his most important works—*On the Track of Unknown Animals*—which was the first of many well-regarded books, including the now famous *In the Wake of the Sea Serpent.*

Heuvelmans's publications sparked interest in cryptozoology not only in scientific communities but also among the general public. He spent most of his adult life circling the globe in search of rare "hidden" creatures. In 1982, he became one of the founding members of the now-defunct International Society of Cryptozoology (ISC) and served as the president until his death in 2001 at age eighty-four.

Plesiosaurs

Tim Dinsdale (1924-1987)

Tim Dinsdale was one of the most dedicated searchers for the Loch Ness Monster. Between 1960 and 1987, he embarked on fifty-six expeditions, most of them solo, and he helped many of the other people who hunted for Nessie during those years.

Dinsdale spent a year analyzing evidence about the Loch Ness Monster's existence. In 1960, with a borrowed camera and on the last day of his first expedition to Loch Ness, he filmed a large object that moved rapidly across—and at times just below the surface of—the water; an object larger than any species known to inhabit the Loch. His footage is now world famous.

Dinsdale spent the rest of his life in pursuit of further evidence that would compel scientific acknowledgement and study of the Loch Ness creatures. He left his career in aeronautical engineering to make his living in ways that allowed him time for fieldwork, but he refused to derive any monetary gain from his work at Loch Ness. He influenced many people, through his example, his lectures, and his books.

Grover Krantz (1931-2002)

Krantz, a notable anthropologist, caused controversy in the scientific community because he was prepared to go out on a limb and say that he believed in Bigfoot. But he also stirred up controversy in the cryptozoology community because he believed it was necessary to kill one of these hairy-hominids in order to confirm its existence. He never got a chance to lay his hands on a Bigfoot but his thorough forensic techniques gave credibility to his work, despite the skepticism of many of his scientific peers.

PATRON OF PIONEERS

In the 1950s, monster hunting was at the height of its popularity, and the numerous expeditions mounted to find hidden animals were largely funded by private individuals. Oil tycoon Tom Slick (1916–1962) was one of the most flamboyant and prominent of these generous benefactors.

Most renowned for his Nepalese expeditions in search of the Yeti, Slick also dedicated generous amounts of time and funding to pursuing Bigfoot, the Loch Ness Monster and other lake monsters, and the giant salamanders of California.

Richard J. Greenwell (1942-2005)

Originally from England, Greenwell spent most of his adult life traveling to far-flung corners of the world looking for hidden animals. He searched for the Mokèlé-mbèmbé (see page 130) in the Congo in the early 1980s, and he led zoological and cryptozoological trips to over thirty countries as diverse as Papua New Guinea, America, Mexico, and China, until he died of cancer in 2005. He was the co-founder and secretary of the ISC from its inception.

One of the most famed of the 1960s Nessie Hunters, Ted Holiday (1920-1979) split opinion within the cryptozoology community with his theories on the Loch Ness Monster's origins. He proposed that the beast, which he called a great worm, was a distant relative of both the octopus and the common garden slug, grown to vast dimensions. According to Holiday, Nessie was in fact an overgrown version of the long extinct, carnivorous invertebrate known as *Tullimonstrum gregarium*.

However, Holiday's work was tarnished in the 1990s as his theories became increasingly extreme. By that stage of his career, he believed that the monsters were not animals at all but conduits for evil forces. He was even involved in an attempt (televised by the BBC) to exorcise the monster of the loch in 1973.

Today's Torch Bearers
Roy Mackal (1925-)

Mackal spent his early career researching biochemistry and virology, but it was on a trip to the United Kingdom in 1965 that he became smitten with the Nessie hunter's bug. He monitored the waters of the Loch and became scientific director of the Loch Ness Investigation Bureau (LNIB). Mackal actually had his own sighting of Nessie in 1970.

His team acquired some sonar signals, which suggested large objects, possibly monsters, in the lake and they also produced some tantalizing underwater photographs that looked remarkably like a massive flipper, but they were unable to provide any conclusive evidence that the Loch Ness Monster(s) existed.

During the 1980s, Mackal turned his attention to another legendary creature, the Mokèlé-mbèmbé, a cryptid allegedly living in the swamps of the Congo. He led two expeditions to the region where he collected important firsthand reports.

As one of the founding members of the now defunct ISC, Mackal is a seminal figure in twenty-first-century cryptozoology.

Loren Coleman (1947-)

Best-selling author, documentary-maker, university lecturer, and field investigator, Loren Coleman is probably the most pre-eminent figure in twenty-first-century cryptozoological research. He has written numerous books on subjects including Anomalous Big Cats, the Yeti, the Sasquatch, and the Mothman; he has also published an encyclopedia entitled

Crypto-zoology: A to Z. Coleman is also one of the few modern cryptozoologists who actually bore witness to the now virtually mythical Minnesota Iceman.

Bigfoot

THE BRITISH COLUMBIA SCIENTIFIC CRYPTOZOOLOGY CLUB

The British Columbia Scientific Cryptozoology Club (BCSCC) is an organization "committed to exploration, research, investigation, and also to maintaining databases on cryptozoological animals from all over the globe."

Founded in 1989 by writer James A. Clark, scientist Paul LeBlond, and journalist John Kirk, the BCSCC has a broad-based membership of enthusiasts who are actively engaged in discovering various animals as yet unidentified by science, in particular the Mokèlé-mbèmbé, lake serpents, the Sasquatch, the Yeti, the Almas of Russia, and the Yeren of China.

As the sole remaining international organization representing cryptozoologists, the BCSCC is determined to be taken seriously by the scientific community in particular, but also by the public at large, stating, "Let it be clearly known that the BCSCC is a scientific body which follows the accepted principles of orthodox zoology in regard to establishing the existence of new species of animals."

Gary Mangiacopra (1960-)

Renowned for his work investigating North American lake monsters, Mangiacopra is also a recognized expert on eighteenth- and nineteenth-century New England sea serpents. He has published several books and articles on Fortean topics ranging from the Rhodesian dinosaur to ufology (see Popular Q&As page 196).

Craig Woolheater (1960-)

As founder and director of the Texas Bigfoot Research Center (TBRC), Woolheater has a place in the annals of modern cryptozoology. Even as a child growing up in the Southern states of the U.S., he had a fascination with strange and unusual phenomena. In 1994, Woolheater and his then girl-friend (now wife) had a sighting of a Bigfoot that reawakened his interest, and, in 1999, in response to an internet ad placed by Luke Gross, enquiring if there was anyone in North Texas interested in researching Bigfoot. Woolheater answered the ad, and together he and Gross set up the TBRC.

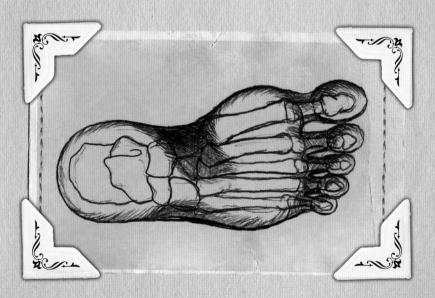

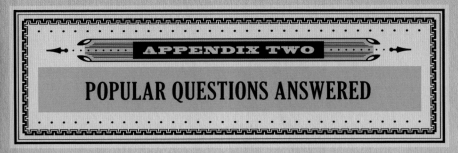

"Extraordinary claims demand extraordinary evidence."
—Marcello Truzzi

Q. What equipment do you need to be a cryptozoologist?

A. This is one of those "how long is a piece of string" questions. If you're a keen crypto-enthusiast sitting on the shores of Loch Ness or backpacking in the Canadian Rockies, then you will only need the most basic of equipment. Apart from the ubiquitous mobile camera-phone, no self-respecting cryptozoologist would leave home without his digital camera, or possibly a video camera and a tape recorder. Many also take plaster with them so that if they come across an interesting footprint, they can pour plaster into a frame to get a cast of the print.

By contrast, well-funded expeditions in search of scientific evidence of cryptids have the most sophisticated equipment available. This ranges from sonar scanners to create pictures of the ocean or lake floor when searching for lake or sea monsters to time-lapse photography and infrared beams to pick up the movements of rare beasts.

Q. How can all these monsters stay hidden despite man's best efforts to find them?

A. It's a good question and one that's vexed cryptozoologists for many years. You might think that with all the advances in surveillance technology such as Global Positioning Systems (GPS), satellite photography, and sonar equipment, there would be nowhere left for cryptids to hide.

But it's obvious to anyone who has ever tried to penetrate the Amazon basin, the Congolese jungle, the Australian Outback, the Sumatran rain forests, the Siberian tundra, or the Himalayan peaks, that there are a multitude of environments on Earth that remain unexplored and virtually impenetrable to man.

Cryptozoologists believe that these remote regions offer enough space and food sources for the survival of a variety of unknown animals that have the elusive skills and camouflage to remain hidden from prying eyes.

Nonetheless, it doesn't change the fact that we are no closer to confirming conclusively the existence of these creatures than we were a hundred years ago. And, unfortunately, the burden of proof lies with the brave and indefatigable souls who still search for these mysterious monsters.

Q. Aren't most mystery creatures just ordinary animals that have been mistaken for something exotic and unknown?

A. Sometimes the long, hard trail to a suspected cryptid ends in disappointment. For example, Richard Greenwell went to Papua New Guinea to investigate claims that a Ri (a sort of mermaid) had been found, only to discover it was a dugong (sea cow). Similarly, the Onza (a mystery cat) turned out to be a subspecies of puma in Mexico.

Most recently, a video showed what was thought to be an ivory-billed woodpecker, an American species believed extinct for more than fifty years, but it was really a pileated woodpecker.

And then, just when you begin to give up hope, a new big cat comes out of the Borneo jungle after 200 years and our faith in cryptids is restored.

So, although mistaken identity does happen on occasion, as Janet Bord, author and co-founder of the Fortean Picture Library, succinctly points out, "...if the skeptics are right and there's no such creature as Bigfoot, then it is a fact that thousands of Americans and Canadians are either prone to hallucinations, or compulsive liars, or unable to recognize bears, deer, and vagrants."

Q. Why are there numerous sightings of a cryptid for a sustained period and then none?

A. Scientists speculate that a change in environment could account for a spate of sightings that then virtually die out. For example, in the case of the Gloucester Sea Monster, there were hundreds of sightings in the late nineteenth and early twentieth century but these have dwindled to virtually none in more recent years. J. P. O'Neill, author of *The Great New England Sea Serpent*, theorizes that the deterioration of the once-fertile fishing areas off the coast of New England by over-fishing may have caused the creature to find another place to eat, or even to become extinct. The same theory can be applied to other cryptozoological creatures.

Q. Is cryptozoology a dying science?

A. Even if investigators found conclusive evidence tomorrow of every cryptid under investigation, who is to say that there are not more unknown animals to be discovered? And in that sense, cryptozoology will always have a place in science.

In addition, there is a small branch of cryptozoology that some believe holds the future for the science, and that involves the possibility of restoring vanished species to life through the extraordinary new possibilities offered by advances in technologies such as DNA extraction and cloning. If you wonder what that means, think about the film *Jurassic Park* and you get the gist.

Once in a while, the Siberian tundra disgorges a frozen mammoth carcass in virtually pristine condition. Perhaps it perished when it fell into a crevasse about 40,000 years ago and now its well-preserved body is a source of tenable genetic material for the possible cloning of a race of rehabilitated "woolly monsters."

Mammoth skeleton

GLOSSARY

A

Aboriginal - People who have inhabited the region from the beginning, i.e. Native Americans and the earliest inhabitants of Australia.

Alien - Not contained in or deriving from the essential nature of something. However, in cryptozoological terms, usually meaning not from Earth.

Amphibian - Amphibians (meaning "double life") are vertebrate animals (with a backbone) that live in the water during their early life (breathing through gills), but usually live on land as adults (and breathe with lungs).

Anthropology - The scientific study of the origin, the behavior, and the physical, social, and cultural development of humans.

Aquatic - Water-dwelling.

B

Basilosaurus - A primitive, extinct whale from 50 million years ago.

Bipedal - A creature that walks on two legs.

C

Carnivore - A creature that eats meat, usually possessing sharp teeth and powerful jaws.

Cetaceans - Marine mammals including toothed whales and toothless, filter-feeding (baleen) whales.

Cryptid - A creature not yet proven to be real.

Cryptobotany - The study of plants which are not currently known to science, but which may have living examples.

Cryptozoology - The search for and scientific study of animals whose existence is unproven, ranging from Bigfoot to Nessie (the Loch Ness Monster).

Cryptozoologist - A scientist or enthusiast who studies cryptozoology.

D

Dinosaurs - (meaning "fearfully great lizard") Land dwelling reptiles that walked with an erect stance during the Mesozoic Era.

E

Extinct - A species no longer existing or living.

Eyewitness reports - First-hand accounts of an event that the person saw or heard themselves.

F

Fortean - Anomalous phenomena, i.e. observed events that lay outside the accepted theories and beliefs of the time.

G

Gigantopithecus - The biggest primate that ever lived roughly one million years ago.

H

Herbivore - A creature that only eats plants.

Hominid - The group describing humans and our close ancestors and relatives.

Hominoidea - The Superfamily Hominoidea includes the apes and humans. It includes the Family Hominidae (people and our close ancestors and relatives), Family Pongidae (orangutans, chimps and gorillas), and Family Hylobatidae (gibbons and siamangs).

L

Loch - A Scottish lake that is home to the Loch Ness Monster.

M

Mammals - Hairy warm-blooded animals that nourish their young with milk.

Marine - Sea-dwelling.

Marsupials - Non-placental mammals (of the order Marsupialia), including kangaroos, opossums, bandicoots and wombats, found principally in Australia and the Americas.

Mesozoic - The Mesozoic Era ("The Age of Reptiles"), occurred from 248-65 million years ago. It is divided into the Triassic, Jurassic, and Cretaceous periods.

N

Nocturnal - A creature that sleeps during the day and is active at night.

O

Oral History - A history recorded orally. Many preliterate cultures relied on oral histories to learn about their past.

P

Paranormal - Beyond the range of normal experience or scientific explanation.

Paleontology - The branch of biology that studies the forms of life that existed in former geologic periods, chiefly by studying fossils. "Paleo" means old or ancient. "Ontology" is the study of existence.

Paleontologist - A scientist who studies paleontology, chiefly by studying fossils.

Plesiosaur - (Meaning "near lizard"). Marine reptiles from the Mesozoic Era who were not considered dinosaurs.

Predator - An animal that hunts and kills other animals for food.

Primate - A creature that uses its access thumb (opposable thumbs), and makes and/or uses tools.

Pterodactyls - Pterodactyls or pterodactyloids (meaning "winged finger") were flying, prehistoric reptiles. They were not dinosaurs.

Pygmy - Unusually small.

Q

Quadrupedal - A creature walking on four legs.

R

Reptiles - The term reptile (meaning "to creep") is loosely defined in everyday English to mean scaly, cold-blooded, egg-laying animals.

S

Sauropod - Huge, quadrupedal, herbivorous dinosaurs with long necks, small heads, and long tails. From the Jurassic or Cretaceous period.

Sighting - The act of catching sight of something, especially something unusual or searched for (in the context of this book – a cryptid).

U

UFO - ("Unidentified Flying Object"). Includes any aerial object that a witness is unable to identify.

Ufology - The study of UFOs and their sightings.

Z

Zoologist - A biologist that studies animals and animal life.